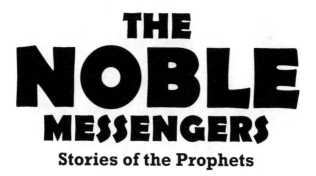

THE NOBLE MESSENGERS

Stories of the Prophets

S. J. SEAR

Illustrations by Khaleel Muhammad

authorHOUSE®

AuthorHouse™ UK
1663 Liberty Drive
Bloomington, IN 47403 USA
www.authorhouse.co.uk
Phone: UK TFN: 0800 0148641 (Toll Free inside the UK)
        UK Local: (02) 0369 56322 (+44 20 3695 6322 from outside the UK)

Published by AuthorHouse 01/07/2022

ISBN: 978-1-6655-9553-7 (sc)
ISBN: 978-1-6655-9552-0 (e)

Contents

Source Books:

* The Noble Qur'an, English translation, King Fahd Complex, Medina.

* Stories of the Prophets by Ibn Kathir.

* The Glory of Muhammad (PBUH) by Mian Abid Ahmad.

* Muhammad (PBUH) The Final Messenger by Dr. Majid Ali Khan.

* Ma'ariful Qur'an by Maulana Mufti Muhammad Shafi.

Foreword

"Allah chooses Messengers from angels and from men." Holy Qur'an, 22: 75.

However, since Allah made the earth a dwelling place for humanity, He chose men, not angels, to be His noble Messengers: "If there were angels walking on the earth ...We should certainly have sent down an angel from heaven as a Messenger." Holy Qur'an, 17: 95.

Like ordinary men, the Messengers married and had children. Some even had troublesome wives, errant sons, or idolatrous parents; but despite personal misfortune the Messengers were endowed with amazing qualities – Nuh's resolute steadfastness, Yusaf's exemplary virtue, Ayyub's infinite patience, Dawud's indomitable courage, and Sulaiman's remarkable wisdom, to name just a few. And from the very first Messenger, Adam (alayhi as-salaam – peace be upon him), to the last Messenger, Muhammad ﷺ (sallallahu alayhi wa-sallam – peace and praise of Allah be upon him), they all shared the same unwavering faith and proclaimed the same Message – belief in the Oneness of God, Almighty Allah, and total submission to His will and commands; the essential tenets of Islam. And despite fierce opposition, extreme adversity, ridicule, rejection, even threat of death, their singular mission was to deliver this Divine Message to humanity.

"We never sent a Messenger except with the language of his people, so that he might make the Message clear to them." Holy Qur'an, 14: 4.

Of the twenty-five Messengers mentioned in the Holy Qur'an, Allah attributes to only five of them strong will, a vital prerequisite for the unique tasks assigned specifically to them. They are Ibrahim, Musa, Nuh, Isa and Muhammadﷺ sallallahu alayhi wa sallam.

The Noble Messengers is a unique journey through time, rediscovering the stories of the noble prophets acknowledged in the Holy Qur'an, beginning with Adam, alayhi as-salaam, and ending with the Last Messenger, Muhammad ﷺ sallallahu alayhi wa-sallam.

"Muhammad ... is the Messenger of Allah and the Seal of the Prophets." Holy Qur'an, 33: 40.

Through the lives of these noble Messengers, their struggles, hardships, and teachings, we learn how we may achieve success in this life and in the Hereafter.

"Indeed, in their stories there is a lesson for men of understanding." Holy Qur'an, 12: 111.

"And We send not Messengers but as givers of glad tidings and to warn you. So, whosoever believes and does virtuous deeds, upon such shall come no fear nor shall they grieve." Holy Qur'an, 6: 48.

The Most Beautiful Names

Since belief in Allah and His Oneness is the essence of the Divine Message conveyed by all His Noble Messengers, this chronicle fittingly begins with a list of the magnanimous names and attributes of Allah as revealed in the Holy Qur'an and Hadith. If we memorise them, we can then call Him by them when we pray.

"And your God is One God; none has the right to be worshipped but He; the Infinitely Merciful, the Lord of Mercy." Holy Qur'an, 2: 163.

"He is Allah, the Creator, the Originator and the Fashioner. To Him belong the most beautiful names ..." Holy Qur'an, 59: 24.

"The most beautiful names belong to God, so call Him by them." Holy Qur'an, 7: 180.

God has countless names that describe His attributes, ninety-nine of which are revealed in the Holy Qur'an and Hadith. The most frequently used name is *Allah*, which is a contraction of the Arabic *al-Ilah*, which means, *the God*.

God's names have a unique expanse and depth of meaning in the Arabic language, so it is impossible to accurately translate them into English, or any other language; and the English spellings inevitably vary according to the translator. Notwithstanding, here are the ninety-nine known Names of Allah with their meanings.

ar-Rahman
The Lord of Mercy

ar-Rahim
The Bestower of Mercy

al-Malik
The Absolute Ruler

al-Quddus
The Holy, Divine

as-Salaam
The Source of Peace

al-Mu'min
The Guardian of Faith

al-Muhaymin
The Protector

al-Aziz
The Honourable

al-Jabbar
The Compeller

al-Mutakabbir
The Majestic, Supreme

al-Khaliq
The Creator

al-Bari
The Evolver

al-Musawwir
The Fashioner

al-Alim
The All-Knowing

al-Qabid
The One Who Restrains

al-Basit
The One Who Enriches

al-Khafid
Giver of Honour or
Shame

ar-Rafi
The Promoter, Exalter

al-Muizz
The Bestower of Honour

al-Muzill
The One Who
Humiliates

as-Sami
The All-Hearing

al-Basir
The All-Seeing

al-Hakam
The Judge, Arbitrator

al-Adl
The Completely Just

al-Latif
The Subtle, Gentle One

al-Khabir
The All-Aware

al-Kabir
The Great

al-Hafiz
The Preserver

al-Muqit
The Maintainer

al-Hasib
Who Takes Account

al-Jalil
The Exalted, Majestic

al-Karim
The Generous One

al-Raqib
The Watchful One

al-Mujib
The Responder to
Prayer

al-Wasi
The Vast,
All-Embracing

al-Hakim
The Wise

al-Wadud
The Loving One

al-Majid
The All Glorious One

al-Ba'ith
The One Who
Resurrects

al-Ghaffar
The All-Forgiving

al-Qahhar
The One Who
Subdues

al-Wahhab
The Generous Giver

ar-Razzaq
The Provider

al-Fattah
Opener, Giver of
Victory

al-Wali
The Protecting Friend

al-Hamid
The Praiseworthy

al-Muhsi
The Appraiser

al-Mubdi
The Originator

al-Mu'id
The Restorer

al-Muhyi
The Giver of Life

al-Mumit
The Giver of Death

al-Halim
The Forbearing One

al-Azim
The Magnificent

al-Ghafur
The All-Forgiving

ash-Shakur
The Appreciative

al-Ali
The Sublime

al-Muqaddim
The Promoter

al-Mu'akhkhir
The Delayer

al-Awwal
First, Without Beginning

al-Akhir
The Last, Without End

az-Zahir
The Manifest, Evident

al-Batin
The Hidden

al-Waali
Patron, Friendly Lord

ash-Shahid
The Witness

al-Haq
The Truth, Reality

al-Wakil
The Reliable Trustee

al-Qawi
The Most Strong

al-Matin
The Firm, Steadfast

al-Muqsit
The Equitable

al-Jame'
The Gatherer

al-Ghani
The Rich,
Independent One

al-Mughni
The Enricher,
Emancipator

al-Mani'
The Preventer of
Harm

ad-Darr
Controller of Benefit,
Harm

al-Nafi
Full of Promise and
Favour

al-Haye
The Ever Living One

al-Qayyum
The Subsisting,
Guardian

al-Wajid
The Unfailing,
Perceiver

al-Majid
The Glorified One

al-Wahid
The Unique One

al-Ahad
The One, the
Indivisible

as-Samad
The Eternal,
Self-Sufficient

al-Qadir
The Able, Capable

al-Muktadir
The Dominant,
Powerful

al-Muta'ali
The Supreme, Most High

al-Barr
The Source of All Good

al-Tawaab
The Acceptor of
Repentance

al-Muntaqim
The Avenger

al-Afuw
The Pardoner

ar-Ra'uf
The Kind, Sympathetic

Malik-ul-Mulk
Eternal Sovereign Lord

Dhul-Jalal Wal-Ikram
Lord of Majesty and
Bounty

an-Nur
The Light

al-Hadi
The Guide

al-Badi
Incomparable
Originator

al-Baqi
The Everlasting

al-Warith
The Supreme
Inheritor

ar-Rashid
Guide to the Right
Path

as-Sabur
The Patient, Steadfast

Prophet Adam

(alayhi as-salaam – peace be upon him)

Allah created the world, the heavens, and the earth. He made angels from light and jinn from smokeless fire. When Allah told the angels He was going to place generation after generation of mankind on the earth they were deeply perturbed.

"Will You place on earth those who will make mischief and shed blood," they asked, "while we glorify You with praises and thankfulness?"

"Surely, I have knowledge that you do not," Allah replied. "So, when I have fashioned him and breathed into him the soul that I created for him, bow down before him."

Allah then fashioned the first man from clay and called him Adam. When He had taught Adam the names of everything, He commanded the angels to bow down to him. All obeyed except the chief jinn, Azazil, who was also present at the time.

For his loyalty and good conduct, Allah had raised Azazil to a status higher than the angels, but he strongly resented the creation of Adam, and extreme pride led him to believe it was not incumbent on him to bow before him. Thereafter, he became known as Iblis, which means, *one without hope.*

"O Iblis, what is wrong with you? Why did you not bow down with the others?" Allah asked.

"I am not one to bow down to a being You created from ordinary clay," was his arrogant reply. "You created me first, and You created me from fire."

"Then get out!" Allah ordered him. "From now on you are an outcast and upon you is a curse until the Day of Judgement."

"O my Lord! Because You have misled me, give me respite till the day when the dead shall be raised again," said Iblis. "And since You have banished me, I shall make all that is evil seem good to mankind and I shall certainly beguile them into grievous error, save those who are truly Your servants and follow You. And You will see, more will follow me."

"You shall have no power over my creatures," Allah told him, "except those who decide to follow you. The truth is, and I speak only the truth, I will fill Hell with you and those who follow you, and the seven gates leading to Hell will each receive its allocated share of sinners."

Allah wanted Adam to have a companion so, from one of Adam's ribs, He created a woman and called her Hawwa (Eve).

"O Adam! Live with your wife in Paradise and eat freely to your heart's content of everything there, but do not come near this tree," said Allah. "And beware of Iblis. Truly, he is your enemy, so do not listen to him."

Still lurking in Paradise, Iblis was watching, listening, and waiting for the first opportunity to lead Adam and Hawwa astray. Drawing close to them, he whispered, "O Adam! Let me show you the Tree of Eternity and Everlasting Kingdom." And he led them to the very tree Allah had forbidden them to touch.

"Truly, I am your sincere friend and well-wisher," he lied. "This tree is only forbidden because its fruit will make you immortal or turn you into angels."

Tempted by the delicious-looking fruit and swayed by Iblis's enticing words, they forgot Allah's warning and tasted the fruit of the forbidden tree; and for the first time, they realised they were completely naked. Deeply ashamed, they gathered leaves and covered themselves.

"Did I not forbid you to touch this tree?" Allah reprimanded. "And did I not warn you that Iblis is not your friend but your enemy? Now, get down from here, all of you, enemies of one another. On earth there will be a dwelling place for you and enjoyment for a time."

Unlike Iblis, who was unremorseful after audaciously disobeying His Creator, Adam and Hawwa were deeply troubled and truly repentant.

"Our Lord!" they cried. "We have wronged ourselves. If You do not forgive us and show mercy we shall certainly be of the losers." And Allah, The Forgiving, The Infinitely Merciful, forgave them.

And so it was that life in Paradise ended and life on earth began. But unlike the tranquillity of Paradise, life on earth was beset with toil and tribulation. To begin with, Adam and Hawwa lost one another and wandered off in different directions. Imagine the trauma of finding themselves lost and alone in an unfamiliar land! And then imagine the ecstasy when, after years of wandering and searching, they finally found one another on a hill now known as the Mount of Mercy!

They built a home for themselves and had children, successive sets of non-identical twins, one boy, one girl; and when their children grew up, they intermarried and had children of their own. Thus, the children of Adam and Hawwa multiplied.

Qabil (Cain) and Habil (Abel) were the first two sons born to Adam and Hawwa, Qabil from the first set of twins, Habil from the second. But like most siblings they were not alike in habits and temperament. Qabil was proud and hot-tempered. Habil was modest, gentle, and mindful of God.

When they reached maturity, the two brothers became engaged in a fierce dispute. Since there were only siblings to marry, Allah inspired Adam with a religious law prohibiting the marriage between a boy and his own twin sister. It so happened that the girl born with Qabil was beautiful, whereas the girl born with Habil was not. In fact, she was quite ugly, but according to the law, Qabil was bound to marry her. Qabil stubbornly refused and insisted on marrying his own twin sister.

To resolve the matter, Adam proposed they both offer a sacrifice to Allah to decide who would have the right to marry the beautiful girl. Qabil, who tilled the land, offered grain as a sacrifice. Habil owned a flock of sheep and presented a lamb. A fire came from the sky and devoured Habil's lamb, a sure sign in those days that God had accepted his sacrifice. Qabil's grain remained untouched. This rejection of his sacrifice so enraged Qabil, he lunged at his brother and threatened to kill him.

"Allah accepts the sacrifice of those who are righteous," Habil calmly explained, "but if you raise your hand to kill me, I shall not raise my hand against you because I fear Allah, Lord of the worlds. Let the sin be on you, not me."

Unable to control his rage, Qabil set upon Habil and killed him. When his temper abated, he stared in horror at his brother's lifeless body and wondered what to do with it; how and where to hide it? Allah then sent a crow that began scratching the ground with its claws, showing him how to bury it.

"How pathetic!" thought Qabil, "I didn't know how to bury a corpse. I had to learn it from a crow."

Qabil soon deeply regretted his wicked deed, but it could not be undone. As a result, Allah decreed that if anyone kills a person, not in retaliation for murder, but to spread mischief in the land, it is as if he kills all humanity; and if anyone saves a life, it is as if he saves the life of all humanity.

So, this is how man's life on earth began, with trouble and hardship, defiance, anger, and bloodshed; a life ever since beset by difficulties and plagued by the devil from all directions. Ultimate success and contentment are only achievable by following the Commands of Allah.

". . . . Surely, there will come guidance from Me, then whoever follows My guidance, no fear shall come upon them, nor shall they grieve." Holy Qur'an, 2: 38.

Author's Comments

The Purpose of Life:
Do you ever wonder what this life is about, its purpose, and why God put us on this earth? Some may conclude this life is a conundrum we do not have the acumen to solve. Or they might feel that life is too great a struggle. They might even succumb to depression and despair. But our earthly life is not a conundrum. Allah has provided us with answers and clear explanations in the Holy Qur'an.

Life Is a Test:
"Do you think that you will enter Paradise before Allah tests those of you who fought (in His cause), and also tests those who are steadfast?" Holy Qur'an, 3: 142.

Life Is for Worship:
"And I (Allah) created not the jinn and mankind except to worship Me." Holy Qur'an, 51: 56.

Life Ends Where It Began:
"Did you think We created you in play (without any purpose), and that you would not be brought back to Us?" Holy Qur'an, 23: 115.

If we follow this simple modus operandi: to worship Allah and all that it encompasses, it becomes the pivotal point of our lives, generating not only contentment, but the courage and strength to cope with all circumstances, thereby ensuring ultimate success. We are all born with a desire to worship and follow Allah, the only path that will lead us back to Him, but oftentimes our quest for the perfect life, here and now, distracts us and may even cause us to falter in our faith and yield to frustration, disappointment, and despair. The perfect life is not here and now, but in the Hereafter, for those who worship and follow Him.

Beware of the Devil:
It only adds to our frustration that we have the devil to contend with. Adam became aware of Iblis's cunningness when he led him astray in Paradise. He learned first-hand, before his role on earth began, that Iblis was the one to look out for.

Iblis gives us good reasons for doing wrong. Just as he enticed Adam and Hawwa to eat the fruit of the forbidden tree with the promise of eternal life, he creeps into every crevice of our hearts and minds and entices us to follow him. And to make matters worse, the devil is not alone.

"Verily, he (the devil) and his soldiers from the jinn or his tribe (Qabiluhu) see you from where you cannot see them." Holy Qur'an, 7: 27.

Iblis had the audacity to blame Allah when he said, "Because You have misled me ..." And that is what those who follow the devil do – blame others for their problems and their sins.

The devil wants us to be miserable. He encourages us to worry unnecessarily. Often, we worry because we are misguided, even arrogant, to believe we have the wisdom and power to solve our problems; and when we cannot find a solution, worry inevitably leads to despair. But worry undermines our faith. It deludes us into believing we are in control when control belongs to Allah alone. *La hawla wala quwwata illa billah* – there is no power nor strength except with Allah. Those who have strong faith depend on Allah to help and guide them. They have only one worry: "Are we doing our best to follow, obey, and please Allah?"

Never despair! For if the devil is there to misguide us, Allah is there to show us the way.

"Verily, the right path has become distinct from the wrong path. Whoever disbelieves in the worship of false gods and believes in Allah, he has grasped the most trustworthy handhold that will never break." Holy Qur'an, 2: 256.

If we turn our backs on the devil and keep a balance between worship, work, and play, we can hope for Allah's Mercy and a place in Paradise.

Beware of Pride:
Pride incites us to quarrel. It prevents us from admitting our mistakes and apologising. And it can lead us to fight, even kill. Pride is the great barrier that separates us from Allah. It causes us to forget or ignore His command to worship Him alone and submit to His will. It is also a thief that can rob us of peace of mind and heart, and of a place in Paradise. It is a gift from the devil; one we must refuse.

Beware of Disobedience and Hope for Forgiveness:
Allah made Iblis an outcast, not only because he refused to obey the command to bow down to Adam, but because he was arrogant and felt no remorse. When Adam and Hawwa ate the fruit of the forbidden tree they also disobeyed Allah. The fruit caused them no physical harm when they ate it, although it revealed their nakedness; but they had failed the most important test, that of obedience to Allah. But because they repented, in His Infinite Mercy Allah pardoned them.

Allah will forgive us, too, if we truly repent. It is also important that we forgive ourselves, as well as others.

"Despair not of the Mercy of Allah: verily, Allah forgives all sins. Truly, He is Oft-Forgiving, Most Merciful." Holy Qur'an, 39: 53.

"Allah does not forgive the setting up of partners with Him (in worship), but apart from that He forgives (anything else) for whom He wills; and whoever sets up partners with Allah has indeed fabricated a tremendous sin." Holy Qur'an, 4: 48.

"If you avoid the great sins which are forbidden, We shall pardon you your small sins and admit you to a Noble Entrance (Paradise)." Holy Qur'an, 4: 31.

What are the great sins? As listed in the Holy Qur'an and Hadith, they include: joining partners in worship with Allah; being undutiful to one's parents; the practice of sorcery (black magic); committing suicide; killing a person, except for a just cause in accordance with Islamic law; giving false witness; taking usury; taking an orphan's property; showing your back to the enemy and fleeing the battlefield; falsely accusing a chaste woman; oppressing the weak and the helpless; unlawful sexual relations outside marriage.

However, in His Infinite Mercy, Allah forgives even the great sins if He Wills.

"And whoever does evil or wrongs himself but afterwards seeks Allah's Forgiveness, he will find Allah Oft-Forgiving, Most Merciful." Holy Qur'an, 4: 110.

The following Hadith was narrated by Abu Hurairah: I heard Allah's Messenger saying, "Allah has divided Mercy into one hundred parts. He has kept ninety-nine parts with Him and sent down one part to the earth; and because of that one part His creatures are merciful to each other, so that even the mare lifts up its hoof away from its baby lest it should trample it."

According to another Hadith narrated by Ibn Abbas, Allah instructed the angels how to record our deeds. If someone intends a virtuous deed, but does not do it, the angels still record that virtuous deed; but if someone intends a virtuous deed and does it, the angel will then record ten to seven hundred virtuous deeds, according to Allah's Mercy. And if someone intends an evil deed, but does not do it, then one virtuous deed will be recorded; and if someone intends an evil deed and does it, only one evil deed will be recorded. Alhamdulillah! So Great is Allah's Mercy!

"Whoever does a virtuous deed shall have ten times the like thereof to his credit; and whoever brings an evil deed shall have only the recompense of the like thereof..." Holy Qur'an, 6: 160.

In the Holy Qur'an, surah 17: 23-38, Allah has clearly set down His commands: to worship none but Him; to be dutiful to parents; to give the kinsman, the wayfarer and the needy their due; not to spend wastefully nor be like a miser; not to kill your children for fear of poverty; not to engage in unlawful sex; not to kill anyone except for a just cause; not to touch the orphan's property except to improve it; to fulfil every covenant; to give full measure; not to give false witness; not to walk arrogantly on earth; for all these sins are hateful to your Lord.

How easy it is to be judgemental, to see the sins and shortcomings of others, but it is not easy to see our own. It is as though sins and shortcomings are written on our back. We can see the sins of others but not our own. So, before we criticise or judge others, we need to reflect, search our own minds and hearts, to discover and acknowledge our own faults. Insha'Allah, if we acknowledge how imperfect we are, then hopefully, that will inspire us to reform and improve. It may also encourage us not to expect perfection in others, and to overlook their mistakes and shortcomings.

Prophet Idris

(alayhi as-salaam – peace be upon him)

Idris was the great grandson of Seth, one of Adam's sons. Born and raised in Babylon, Allah chose him to be a Messenger to his people, to call them back to the religion of their ancestors, but only a small group of men listened. So, Idris left Babylon with his band of faithful followers and settled in Egypt where he continued his mission, teaching the people to pray, fast on certain days and behave righteously and charitably. He encouraged them to give part of their wealth to help the poor and needy. He urged them to worship and obey the One True God.

Idris was the first of the descendants of Adam, after Seth, to be a prophet. Records show that he was the first to invent the basic form of writing. However, little else of authentic origin is known about him except that he was well-known for his wise sayings, like the following:

"Happy is he who looks at his own deeds and appoints them as pleaders to his Lord."

"None can show better gratitude for Allah's favours than he who shares them with others."

"Do not envy people for what they have as they will enjoy it for a time only."

"He who indulges in excess will not benefit from it."

"The real joy of life is to have wisdom."

Prophet Nuh

(alayhi as-salaam – peace be upon him)

After the death of Idris, those who had once followed him turned to evil ways. They forgot Allah and worshipped useless idols instead, so Allah sent Idris's grandson, Nuh, to guide them back to the right path, and to warn them that if they did not leave their wicked ways, Allah would punish them. However, most paid no heed and made fun of him.

"You are just an ordinary man like us," they taunted. "Why should we listen to you? If you do not stop this nonsense, we will stone you to death."

Nuh ignored them and continued to preach even when they carried out their pernicious threats and hurled stones at him until he became unconscious.

"Truly I am a prophet," he bravely insisted. "Allah has sent me to warn you; to tell you to worship none but Him. Obey Allah and He will surely forgive you. He will send rain to water the fields. He will make you prosperous and bless you with children. He will give you flowing rivers and beautiful gardens, but if you do not leave your idols and all your wicked ways, a Day of Disaster will surely come."

"You are a mere mortal like us, and we see no special qualities that merit you above us," the chieftains scoffed. "And see! Only the poor and low-class people follow you."

"I cannot disown my followers simply because they are poor," Nuh calmly replied. "And I am not asking you for any reward, nor do I claim to be an angel or to have knowledge of the unseen."

"Nuh, you have preached long enough," the chieftains curtly interrupted. "And you have only worsened the dispute between us, so bring on this punishment, this calamity you keep threatening us with, if indeed it is true."

Forever calm and steadfast, Nuh replied, "Only Allah will bring it upon you, if He wills, and there will be no escape. I am innocent of all your accusations. I have only delivered Allah's Message."

Each waking hour, Nuh pleaded with his people to follow him. He went to their homes to preach to them in secret, and he preached to them in the open marketplaces. Wherever he went, he preached, hoping they would listen and believe in him and his Message from God, but in their obstinacy and brazenness they turned a deaf ear.

Sad and disheartened, Nuh prayed: "O my Lord! I have called my people and given them Your Message. Time and again, I have called them to follow Thee, but they pay no heed. Every time I tell them You might still forgive them, they put their fingers in their ears, cover their heads with their garments and refuse to listen. They are proud. They call me a madman. They even threaten to kill me."

"I ask them, 'What is wrong with you? You neither fear Allah's punishment nor desire His reward. Don't you know Allah is your Creator? He created you from the dust of the earth to which you will return. He created the seven heavens with the moon a light and the sun a lamp.' Still, they refuse to listen. They say they will never abandon their gods and the worship of their idols, Wadd, Suwa, Yaguth, Ya'uq and Nasr."

"O Nuh!" Allah replied. "Don't be sad because of what they say and do. The few who were destined to believe have already believed. The rest will never believe. So, build the ship as I have commanded you."

Nuh had never built a ship before, so Allah assured him of His help. "Make the ship according to Our revelations," He said.

Nuh then chopped down trees, sawed them into planks and began building the ship in stages, according to Allah's instructions. People gathered around him, curious to know what was happening. Others ridiculed him as they passed by.

"So, all along you've been pretending to be a prophet when in fact you are a carpenter," they taunted. "And what are you doing with all that wood? Building a ship in the blazing desert? And when you have built it, if you ever do, how do you plan to get it to the sea?"

Relentlessly, the disbelievers mocked and jeered, but Nuh ignored them. With true devotion, he continued to worship Allah; and with tenacious energy worked tirelessly to complete the ship in readiness for the impending disaster.

"O my Lord!" he prayed. "Don't leave any of the disbelievers on the earth. If You leave them, they will mislead Your servants and will beget wicked, disbelieving offspring. Spare me and my parents and whoever enters my home as a believer and all the believing people."

At last the ship was ready. Historians claim it was as high as a modern three storey ship, about three hundred yards long, fifty yards wide and thirty yards high. Only Allah knows.

Finally, Allah gave the order to board the ship, saying: "With the name of Allah it sails and reaches land."

Nuh and his family clambered aboard. His three sons, Sam, Ham, and Yafith and their wives, along with his small band of followers and a pair, one male one female of their animals. His disbelieving wife and one of his sons, Yam, were left behind.

Like a tsunami, water gushed from the earth, lifting the ship from its moorings. Rain cascaded from the heavens, and the waters of heaven and earth met in cataclysmic fury. It rained as it had never rained before; and as the ship sailed off,

Nuh's despair; the mighty flood; and survivors.

amidst billowing waves as high as mountains, Nuh caught sight of his wayward son and called out to him.

"O my son! Come with us! Don't stay with the disbelievers!"

But his son neither feared the raging storm nor Allah's wrath. "I shall climb some mountain," he shouted back. "The mountain will save me from the flood."

"O my son!" Nuh cried. "This day, no one will be saved except those who believe in Allah."

Colossal waves like massive mountains then soared between them and swept his son away. And the ship sailed on. And on! How long the floods lasted, only Allah knows. Finally, Allah commanded: "O Earth! Swallow up your water! O Sky! Withhold your rain!"

And as the floodwater subsided, the ship came to rest on Mount Judi. Nuh and all those with him in the ship were safe, but all the disbelievers perished.

Allah had promised Nuh that all his family would be saved, so he still hoped his son might be alive even though he had seen the monstrous waves engulf him.

"O my Lord!" he prayed. "My son was of my family. But Your promise is surely true, and You are the Most Just of Judges."

"O Nuh!" said Allah. "Truly, he was not of your family. He behaved wickedly. So do not ask about something of which you have no knowledge."

Truly repentant, Nuh prayed for forgiveness.

"Come down from the ship, Nuh," Allah commanded, "with peace from Us and blessings on you and all those with you."

So Nuh, together with his family, his little band of followers and all the animals, left the ship to begin a new life in a new land.

Author's Comments

Steadfastness is a quality all prophets possess. But imagine! Prophet Nuh lived 950 years and spent his entire adult life preaching to people who did not believe and refused to follow him, his wife and one of his sons included.

Parents often worry about their children, especially when they do not listen or disobey, or worse, when they go astray. But it is not in anyone's power to protect others or guide those who choose to disbelieve. Only Allah has the power. *La hawla wala quwwata illa billah* – there is no power nor strength except with Allah. And no one can carry the burden of another's sins nor share their merit. On the Day of Judgment, Allah will judge everyone according to their own deeds only.

Patience is an integral part of faith, but if someone does not listen to us how impatient we become. How impatient we are when we want something but must wait for it, or when our prayers seem unanswered! Often, we do not even have the patience to wait our turn in a queue. But how patient was Nuh!

He also had unquestionable faith. He never doubted that a Day of Great Disaster would come. Allah had told him so. And during all those years of struggle and strenuous labour, never did he question the wisdom of building a massive ship where there was neither river nor sea; simply because he had complete faith in Almighty Allah Who had commanded him to do so.

Prophet Hud

(alayhi as-salaam – peace be upon him)

Prophet Hud, whose lineage is linked with Prophet Nuh, was the appointed Messenger of the people of Banu 'Ad, who lived in a dusty, hilly region near Hadramout in Yemen. The three sons of Nuh who survived the flood, Sam, Ham and Yafith, scattered and settled in the Arabian Peninsula. Sam had a son named Iram, and one of Iram's sons was Aus, who in turn had a son named 'Ad. Aus then named the place where they lived 'Ad, after his son.

The people of 'Ad were remarkably tall with powerful physique. They were also affluent, blessed with livestock, gardens, fruits, and all kinds of produce. Expert masons and artisans, they hued out houses in the hillside and constructed beautiful temples, magnificent palaces, and tall buildings with lofty towers. They were so proud of their achievements they considered themselves invincible; and so inebriated with affluent living they became depraved, defiant, and oblivious to the fact that their prosperity was not due to their own efforts but to the favour and blessings of Almighty Allah.

Once believers only in the One True God, they had turned to worshipping the stars and false deities, the most important being Saqi'ah, Salimah, Raziqah and Hafizun. They acknowledged Allah's existence. They even worshipped Him. He was the God of their ancestors. But alongside Allah, they worshipped their self-made gods and idols.

If the common citizens were decadent and depraved, those in power were worse. Pompous, unscrupulous dictators whom none dared to raise a voice against for fear of punishment or death. Allah thus endowed Hud, who lived among them, with prophethood. However, like so many nations before them, instead of listening to the prophet's divine Message, they ridiculed him. They denounced him for criticizing their gods and called him a crazy lunatic.

"O my people!" said Hud. "What is the benefit of these stones that you have carved with your own hands? There is only one deity worthy of worship and that is Allah. He created you and will cause you to die. He provides for you. He is the One who gave you superior physique and blessed you in so many ways, so believe in Him and Him alone. Don't take Allah's blessings for granted lest the same dreadful fate that destroyed Nuh's people should befall you."

Hud's pleadings were not only ignored, but one man named Abu Thamud fiercely opposed him and tried to rouse the people against him. He even took it upon himself to prove to everyone that Hud was indeed a lunatic.

"Do you want to be our master or our ruler? Is that your plan?" he asked. "If so, how much do you want to be paid?"

"O my people! I seek no reward for the Message I bring you. My reward is only from Him Who created me. Will you not understand? Repent and ask forgiveness from the Lord. He will send down rain in abundance and increase your strength. Do not turn away as disbelievers."

"O Hud! You have brought us no evidence that might persuade us to believe in you and your Message," the people replied. "We refuse to leave our gods merely on your saying. It seems some of our gods have seized you with evil."

"Allah bears witness that I am free from that which you ascribe as partners with Allah in worship. So, think what you will and give me no respite, my trust is in Allah, my Lord, and your Lord. There is not a living creature, but He has it in His grasp, so if you turn away after I have conveyed His Message the loss will be yours. My Lord will make another nation succeed you. You will not harm Him in the least; you will only harm yourselves. Surely, my Lord is Guardian over all things."

Thus was Hud's bold response, but as before they scoffed at him. He then warned them that if they did not heed his Message a dreadful day would come, a Day of Judgement and Punishment.

Astonishingly, Abu Thamud, who had triggered the people's antagonism, had been evaluating Hud's preaching and was inclined to believe in the God he worshipped. He then tried to persuade others to believe. He began by appealing to their intelligence and common sense, refuting the foolish notion that the statues they made with their own hands could have created the earth and all that it contained.

"Surely, there must be a Higher Being who created all this," he said, urging everyone he knew to believe in the One True God. He advised them to take stock of their lives; the way they wasted their time with idol-worship, gambling, drinking and other useless pursuits.

"Preposterous!" one man retorted. "Abu Thamud is either a raving lunatic or Hud has cast a spell on him."

Undaunted, Abu Thamud was now convinced that Hud preached the truth, so he went to him and declared his faith. Try as they may, the people could not persuade Abdullah to return to idol worship, so they gave up, swearing most adamantly that they would never leave their idols or believe that Hud was a prophet.

"He hasn't come with any signs, so he must be lying," they taunted.

Regardless of their scepticism, Hud pursued his mission, pleading with them to leave their wicked ways before it was too late. He explained that in this lifetime truth is not always victorious nor virtue rewarded, that evil often prevails, and that for crimes to go unpunished would be a great injustice. Allah forbids injustice, so He has appointed a Day of Reckoning when every single person will be rewarded for all his honourable deeds and punished for all his sins.

Most walked away when he preached, but those who did stop to listen only ridiculed him afterwards. And when he reminded them of the dreadful fate of Nuh's people, they simply made fun of Nuh, too.

"Who is going to destroy us?" the chiefs asked tauntingly.

"Allah will!" Hud replied.

"Our gods will save us," they boasted.

Hud shook his head despairingly and sighed, "O my people! The gods you worship will be the very cause of your destruction."

In a final attempt to make them understand, Hud explained that only Allah has power on earth and the power to save them; that their so-called gods, made with their own hands, had no power whatsoever. Still, they paid no heed and the dispute between them continued.

Hud's people became increasingly defiant, mercilessly ridiculing and persecuting him. Now doomed, their punishment would surely come. And come it did!

A terrible drought spread throughout the land. For three long years, there was no rain. Only the burning sun scorching the earth. All the beautiful gardens and fields of crops withered and died. The cattle died, too.

"Why is there a drought?" the people asked Hud.

"Because Allah is angry with you," he replied. "But if you believe in Him, He will send rain and make you strong and prosperous once more."

But as before, they only mocked him, so the drought continued. Parched by the hot sun, the trees also withered and died. Then came a day when the sky was full of massive black clouds.

"Rain!" the people cried in jubilation, believing the terrible drought was about to end. But these were not rain clouds. Thick and ominous, they covered the sky, and the weather suddenly changed from scorching heat to piercing cold. Howling like wild beasts, fierce winds battered the land, and for eight days and seven nights the storm raged mercilessly, tossing people, trees, and debris into the air, decimating everything in its path.

Most tried to escape to the dwellings in the hillside, but the wind caught up with them and showed no mercy. When the cataclysm was over, the entire region lay in ruins. Except for Hud and his followers, all the people of 'Ad perished.

Powerless were those who had brazenly boasted their might. Futile the gods they worshipped. All-Powerful the God they had so adamantly denied.

Hud and his band of faithful followers left the rubble and ruins and migrated to Hadramout where they lived in peace, worshipping the One True God.

Author's Comments

The people of Hud committed a deadly sin – shirk, the worship of other gods besides Allah. And they were guilty of another grave sin – pride.

A true believer is not proud of the way he looks or the way he lives. He knows that good health, wealth, and success in life are blessings from Allah. Each person will depart from this earth, taking nothing but faith and virtuous deeds. Mansions, palaces, lofty buildings, and material comforts will all be left behind. So, we need to be mindful of Allah and to be careful in everything we do.

Prophet Salih

(alayhi as-salaam – peace be upon him)

The tribe of Thamud succeeded 'Ad, and far exceeded them in power and splendour. They were the descendants of Thamud, son of Abir, son of Sam, the son of Nuh. They built lofty buildings on the plains and hewed beautiful homes out of the hills, but like those before them they were proud and decadent and worshipped idols. Evil men ruled, and corruption, cruelty, injustice, and unrest prevailed throughout the land.

Allah then inspired His Messenger, Salih, to guide them to the right path; a man from among them who was already renowned for his wisdom and righteousness. As always, it was not an easy task trying to convince the people to leave their fake gods and worship Allah alone.

"O Salih!" the people said. "We greatly admire you. We even had plans to make you our chief until you started this nonsense about leaving the gods of our ancestors and worshipping your God. You are merely a human being like

The blessed camel, and those who later plotted to kill her.

us, yet you say you are a prophet. So, prove it. Ask your God to send us a sign. Show us a miracle."

"And if Allah sends you a sign, will you believe?" asked Salih.

"Yes," they promised.

So, out of the mountain Allah made a magnificent camel appear that soon proved to be no ordinary camel. Its milk was sufficient for hundreds of people and the other animals abandoned the place where it slept, sure signs that this was indeed a unique, blessed creature. But while some kept their promise and believed in Salih's Message, others went back on their word and continued to disbelieve. They began to harbour ill feelings towards Salih and made the sacred camel the target of their animosity, devising ways to harm her.

Suspecting they might be scheming to kill the sacred camel, Salih warned them. "O my people! This she-camel from Allah is a sign to you, so leave her to graze peacefully. If you harm her, you will be punished."

For a while, they heeded Salih's warning and let the sacred camel drink and graze freely; but soon they began to complain that she drank all the water and frightened their cattle away. Animosity grew in their hearts, and they secretly plotted to kill her.

A group of men, chosen to conduct the dreadful deed, sat down near the well and waited for the camel to come for water. As she drank, one of them shot an arrow and wounded her in the leg. Another rushed upon the fallen creature and struck her in the other leg with his sword. One last thrust of the sword through her body and the camel's life was over.

While everyone celebrated, applauding the killers as heroes, Salih warned them that their end was now near. "Enjoy life for three more days," he said. "Then surely, Allah's wrath will descend upon you."

"Why should we wait three days? Let it come sooner," they mockingly replied.

Salih's heart sank at their recklessness. "O my people! Why do you wish to hasten evil rather than good? Why don't you seek Allah's forgiveness while there's still time, so that you may receive His pardon and mercy?" he pleaded.

A few people responded and joined Salih's band of followers, but most scoffed at his advice and despised him even more. The main mischief-makers were the nine sons of the chiefs of the well-known city of Hijr. They were high-ranking elite, each a leader of his own clan. Together, they swore a secret oath to kill Salih and his followers. They had killed the sacred camel, so why not kill the prophet as well and be rid of this botheration. Unhindered, they would be free to do whatever they wished.

To ensure that no surviving legatee could claim compensation for Salih's death, their plan was to attack at night when it would be virtually impossible for anyone to recognise and later identify them. Unknown to them, however, Allah had forewarned Salih who was already preparing to leave the city.

When the three days had passed, the sky suddenly darkened and huge, black, clouds gathered menacingly overhead. Lightning lit the skies, followed by deafening thunderbolts and furious winds that lacerated the land. Finally, a series of violent tremors shook the earth and totally destroyed the city.

Their strongly built houses, rock-hewn homes and fake gods offered them no protection on that awful day. Such was the fate of the people of Thamud.

Author's Comments

How foolish the people of Thamud! They neither learnt from the awful destruction of those before them nor heeded Salih's warnings. Their downfall was the result of their extreme arrogance and decadence. Throughout history, wealthy, decadent people spent their lives in self-indulgence, committing atrocities with impunity, oblivious of the consequences, and fearless of the Day of Judgement (Yawm al-Din) when no one will escape accountability.

Prophet Ibrahim

(alayhi as-salaam – peace be upon him)

The noble prophet, Ibrahim, lived in the city of Ur among the Chaldean people in the Mesopotamian valleys of the Tigris-Euphrates River systems where the ancient empires of Babylon and Assyria once flourished, today's Iraq, east Syria, and south-east Turkey. The Chaldeans were keen astronomers and worshipped the sun, moon, and stars, as well as idols that represented different heavenly bodies.

As a young man, Ibrahim was deeply troubled by the idol worship that dominated the lives of his people. He was convinced there was a true God, One Who had created everyone and everything in the universe. Eager to learn the truth, he spent many sleepless nights meditating, searching for an answer. One night, he looked up and saw a bright star in the sky.

"This must be my Lord," he said. But when the star set in the sky he sighed, "I do not like a thing that sets. This cannot be my Lord."

When he saw the moon rising, he said, "This must be my Lord." But the moon also set in the sky. "My Lord, guide me," he prayed. "Otherwise, I shall be one of those who go astray."

"Surely, this is my Lord," he said, as he watched the sun rising. "It is much bigger and brighter."

But the sun also set, proving to Ibrahim that the sun, moon, stars, and all the other heavenly bodies that his people worshipped were only part of Allah's creation and subject to His laws.

"And this was Our argument which we gave to Ibrahim against his people." Holy Qur'an, 6: 84.

Ibrahim was now content because Allah had enlightened him. "O my people! I am now free from the sin of which you are guilty, that of belief in idols as partners of Allah. And I have firmly turned towards Him, Creator of the heavens and the earth and everything in it."

However, the people were not pleased by this sudden revelation. To the contrary, they deeply resented Ibrahim's proclamation and threatened to harm him, but he remained calm and unafraid.

"Nothing can happen to me, except by Allah's Will," he said.

Having discovered the true faith, Ibrahim was deeply troubled about his father, Azar, who was a devoted idol-worshipper. Worse still, making idols was his trade and livelihood.

"Why do you worship idols?" he asked him. "They can neither see nor hear you, nor can they help you in any way. Allah has guided me and shown me the right path, so follow me."

Azar exploded with rage. "Do you reject my gods?" he bellowed. "If you dare say another word against them, I will stone you to death."

Realising that nothing could convince his father to abandon idol-worship, Ibrahim promised to pray for him.

"Peace be with you," he said. "I shall beg my Lord to forgive you. He is always gracious to me. But for now, I shall leave you and the idols you all pray to; and I shall pray to my Lord and trust that my prayer is not in vain." Holy Qur'an, 19: 47, 48.

Ibrahim then left his father. He continued to preach, hoping others would listen and follow him. He even went to Nimrud, the King of Babylon, and preached to him.

"Worship Allah, for it is Allah who gives life and causes death," he said.

Nimrud was furious. No one had ever dared to speak to him like this. He was not only king of his people; he was their god.

"No! You are wrong!" he retorted. "It is I who give life and cause death."

True, he was a cruel king and frequently sentenced prisoners to death, so Ibrahim presented him with a different argument.

"Truly, Allah causes the sun to rise from the east. If you are more powerful, then cause it to rise from the west."

Clearly confused, but too proud to admit it, Nimrud refused to listen further. He was the king. No one had the right to tell him what to do, and no one could ever convince him and his people to renounce their precious idols.

"When you are not looking, I will destroy all your idols," Ibrahim told him, fully intending to carry out his threat, though not sure how or when because the temple was always crowded with idol worshippers.

One day, however, he noticed people were leaving the temple to attend a pagan feast outside the city.

"Come with us, Ibrahim," they invited. "Come and join in the feast."

This was the chance Ibrahim had been waiting for. As an excuse to stay behind, he pretended to be unwell; and when he was sure everyone had left, he quietly slipped into the temple.

"Why don't you eat the offering before you?" he taunted the idols. "And what is the matter with you that you do not speak? Why do you not reply?"

He then turned on them and with his right hand smashed them all except the biggest. Placing an axe on the biggest idol's shoulder, he left the temple as surreptitiously as he had entered.

The broken idols in the temple.

There was utter pandemonium when the people returned. Wailing loudly, they ran from one idol to another, wringing their hands and beating their heads. Suddenly, one of them remembered Ibrahim's words.

"He threatened to destroy our idols. He must have done this."

But when they confronted Ibrahim, he boldly lied and denied it. "I did not break your idols. The biggest one did. Ask the others. They will tell you."

"You know very well they cannot talk," was their foolish but honest reply.

"Then why do you worship them?" Ibrahim asked. "Do they hear you when you call them? Can they help or harm you in any way?"

"No," they answered, "but our fathers and forefathers worshipped them."

"O my people! It is Allah Who created me, guides me, feeds me, and gives me drink. When I am ill, it is He who cures me. He will cause me to die and bring me back to life again. Only He can forgive me. So, worship Allah alone," Ibrahim implored. "That is better for you."

This was too much. He had broken their idols and now he was pleading with them to give up their religion.

"Build a furnace and throw him into it!" Nimrud ordered.

And as the guards grappled with Ibrahim, the crowd burst into chorus, chanting, "Burn him! Burn him!"

They threw Ibrahim into the blazing fire, but he did not struggle or cry out. He remained calm and prayed, *"Hasbi Allahu wa naima al-Wakeel."* Allah is sufficient for us, and He is the Best Disposer of Affairs.

Allah then commanded, "O fire, be cool and protect Ibrahim!"

The people could not believe their eyes when he walked from the fire, completely unharmed. But strange as it may seem, even then they refused to believe and follow him.

"I am going to my Lord," Ibrahim told them. "He will guide me." And he travelled far, through Babylon, Assyria, Egypt, and other lands, preaching to everyone he met along the way.

One day, he prayed, "My Lord! Show me how You give life to the dead."

"Why? Do you not believe?" Allah asked.

"Yes, I believe, but I ask just to satisfy my heart," Ibrahim replied.

"Take four birds and train them to come to you," Allah told him. "Place a part of them on every mountain and then call them. They will come to you flying. And know that Allah is Mighty, Wise."

Ibrahim married a beautiful woman named Sarah, but for years they remained childless. So, Sarah persuaded him to marry her Egyptian maidservant, Hajarah, and Allah blessed them with a son. They named him Isma'il. Sarah, however, soon became extremely jealous of them and asked Ibrahim to send them far away.

Deeply troubled by her request, Ibrahim was reluctant to comply, but then Allah commanded him to do as Sarah asked, assuring him that Hajarah and the child would be safe. So, he set off towards Makkah, which at that time was dry, barren, and uninhabited. After making a crude shelter, he left them there with just a bag of dates and an animal-skin bag filled with water to sustain them.

As he set off back home, Hajarah got up and ran after him. "O Ibrahim!" she called. "Where are you going, leaving us alone in this desolate valley where there is no one to keep us company and nothing to enjoy?"

Repeatedly, she called out to him, but Ibrahim walked on. He neither looked back nor replied. Then she called out, "Has Allah ordered you to do this?"

And across the wasteland she heard Ibrahim reply, "Yes!"

"Then He will not neglect us," Hajarah assured herself; and she watched in silence as Ibrahim walked farther and farther away.

Only when he was sure he was out of sight did he look back.

"O Lord!" he prayed. "I have settled my offspring in a barren valley near the ruins of Thy Sacred House. Make this place a secure town and provide its people with fruits; those who believe in Allah and the Last Day."

In the scorching heat, Hajarah soon felt thirsty. When she had drunk the last drop of water, baby Isma'il began to cry inconsolably. She tried to suckle him, to comfort him, but he would not stop crying. Desperately thirsty, and feeling helpless and forlorn, she left him lying on the ground and ran off to find help. She kept running until she came to a hill known as al-Saffa.

Clambering to the top, she looked out over the valley hoping to see a caravan passing by, but there was nothing. So, she tucked her long robe into her belt, scrambled back down the hillside and ran across the valley in the opposite direction until she reached al-Marwah, another hill. She climbed to the top and looked around hoping to be luckier this time, but again there was nothing and no one in sight.

Not knowing what else to do, and still hoping she might find someone to help her, Hajarah kept on running between the two hills. When she reached al-Marwa for the seventh time, she thought she heard someone calling. She stood still to listen; certain she had heard something.

"Whoever you are, I have heard your voice," she called out. "Do you have something to comfort me?"

She then looked down to where she had left Isma'il and was amazed to see an angel standing over him; and as the angel lightly scraped the sand with the tip of its wings, a spring suddenly appeared. She raced down the hillside and tried to hold back the water with her hands.

"Zam! Zam! (Stop! Stop!)" she cried, but the water gushed out with such force she could not stop it. With her bare hands, she dug a basin around it to hold the precious water. After filling the water-skin and quenching her thirst, she sat down to suckle her infant son.

"Don't be afraid of being neglected," the angel comforted her, "for here is the House of Allah, which will be built by your son and his father, Ibrahim. Allah never neglects His people."

Hajarah lived alone with Isma'il near the spring named Zam Zam until one day, a caravan of people from the tribe of Jurham happened to pass nearby. They spotted a bird flying over the valley, one that always flies over water. This is a waterless valley, so why is this bird flying over it, they wondered? Water being an extremely precious commodity in the desert, they immediately sent someone to investigate. When he returned and told them about the spring, they decided to enter the valley. Hajarah was pleased to see them; and when they asked if they could stay, she readily agreed but first made it clear that they had no rights over Zam Zam. So, they settled in the valley and sent for the rest of their families to join them.

Hajarah was delighted to have good people around her. They adored her little son and were impressed by his pleasant nature and gentle ways. Occasionally, Ibrahim also visited them. When Isma'il was about twelve years old, he came and told him, "My son! Three times I have seen in a dream that I should offer you as a sacrifice to Allah. So, tell me, what should I do?"

"O my father! Do what you are commanded," Isma'il calmly replied, "and Insha'Allah, you will find me patient."

Understandably, Ibrahim was deeply perplexed, torn between his love for his son and his desire to please his Lord. To make matters worse, the devil tempted him three times, trying to convince him not to make the sacrifice. Finally, Ibrahim dismissed the devil's cunning arguments and laid Isma'il down.

He was about to slaughter him when Allah spoke: "O Ibrahim! You have fulfilled the dream. It was a great test for you. We shall surely reward you." And He sent a ram, which Ibrahim then killed as a sacrifice.

Time passed, and Isma'il grew into a fine young man. He married a woman from the tribe of Jurham. Ibrahim went to meet him one day, but he was not at home.

"He has gone in search of our livelihood," his wife told him.

"And how is your livelihood?" Ibrahim asked. "What are your circumstances?"

"Miserable," she replied. "We are living in great hardship."

Her reply saddened him. Instead of expressing words of praise and thanks for whatever Allah provided, she had complained. "When your husband returns, please give him my regards and tell him to change the threshold of his home."

Later that day, when Isma'il returned, his wife described the visitor and told him what he had said. "That was my father, and he has ordered me to divorce you, so go back to your people."

Soon after, Isma'il married another woman from the same tribe. Ibrahim went again to visit Isma'il, but as before he was not at home. And when he asked his wife about their livelihood she replied, "By the grace of Allah, we are very well off."

Ibrahim was delighted and asked her to convey his regards to her husband and advise him to keep the threshold of his home. When she told Isma'il, he was pleased. "That was my father, and he has ordered me to keep you with me, for you are the blessing of my home."

Several years later, Ibrahim again went to Makkah to see his son. He found him sitting beneath the shade of a tree near Zam Zam, sharpening his arrows. After affectionately greeting one another, Ibrahim said, "My son! Allah has given me an order."

"Then do what your Lord has ordered," Isma'il replied with his usual serenity.

"Allah has ordered me to build His House here," said Ibrahim, pointing to a hillock nearby. "Will you help me?"

Together, Ibrahim and Isma'il began building the House of Allah, the Holy Kaaba, just as the angel had foretold; and as they worked, they prayed: "Our Lord! Accept this service from us. Truly, You are the All-Hearing, the All-Knowing. Make us devoted to You and from our offspring make a nation devoted to You. Show us how to worship You and accept our repentance, for You are the Ever Relenting, the Most Merciful. Our Lord! Make a Messenger of their own rise from among them; to recite Your revelations to them, teach them the scripture and wisdom, and purify them. You are the Exalted in Might, The Wise."

Years later, Allah answered this prayer when Prophet Muhammad ﷺ sallallahu-alayhi-wa sallam, a direct descendant of Isma'il, was born.

Ibrahim spent the rest of his life in the fertile land of Canaan (Palestine) where he established a city named Jerusalem. The people of the city and all the surrounding areas accepted his religion and became his followers. When they asked him for a place of worship, Ibrahim placed a sacred stone in the centre of the city to mark the place of worship.

One day, three visitors came to his house, and he welcomed them as he would any honoured guests. He prepared a roasted calf for them, but when they declined the meal he began to feel uneasy. It turned out, however, that these were no ordinary visitors. They were angels, the angel Jibril and two others, who had come to give him good news of a son.

How is that possible, Ibrahim questioned? He was about one hundred years old, and his wife was in her late nineties, way beyond child-bearing age. Astonished at the news, Sarah cried aloud and slapped her face.

"Do you wonder at Allah's decree?" the angels asked.

Sarah gave birth to a baby boy whom they named Ishaq (Isaac). When he was just eight days old, Allah directed Ibrahim to circumcise him and all other males in the family, a practice upheld today among Jews and Muslims throughout the world.

Ishaq grew into a strong, handsome young man and married Ribika (Rebecca) who bore him twin sons, Eisu (Esau) and Yakub (Jacob). Eisu abandoned the faith and went his own way. Yaqub was the ancestor of the great line of Prophets – Yusaf, Musa, Dawud, Sulaiman and Isa.

Author's Comments

Ibrahim's people were obsessed with the worship of heavenly bodies, the sun, moon, and stars. In the Holy Qur'an, 6: 97, it says: "It is He Who has set the stars for you so that you may guide your course with their help through the darkness of the land and the sea."

And the following is Hadith by Sahih al-Bukhari: The creation of the stars is for three purposes – as decoration of the nearest heaven, as missiles to hit the devils, and as signs to guide travellers. If anybody tries to find a different interpretation, he is mistaken and merely wastes his efforts, and troubles himself with what is beyond his limited knowledge.

Ibrahim's father was adamant in his disbelief in Allah, but that is the choice we all have, to believe or not to believe; to follow Allah or to go our own way. What the angel said to Hajarah should help us make the right choice – the promise that Allah never neglects His people. More than that, He rewards them.

From Isma'il, we learn how to be completely obedient to the Will of Allah, and to our parents. His faith was unshakable when Allah asked Ibrahim to sacrifice him; and when it was a question of his marriage, he had total confidence in his father's judgement. Both wives lived in the same conditions, but his first wife dwelt on her hardship while the second counted her blessings. If asked about our circumstances, how would we reply?

We all know Allah is *Al-Wali*, our Protecting Friend, but did you know that Allah called Ibrahim *Khalilullah*, Allah's Intimate Friend?

"And God did take Ibrahim for an intimate friend." Holy Qur'an, 4: 125.

In the Qur'an, Allah also refers to him as *Hanif*, a true believer in the Oneness of God. What an honour! One we may never attain but can certainly strive for.

Here is one of Ibrahim's prayers: "Our Lord, do not punish us if we forget or make a mistake. Our Lord! Do not place on us a burden like that You placed on those before us. Our Lord! Do not place on us a burden we have not the strength to bear. Pardon us, forgive us and have mercy on us." Holy Qur'an, 2: 286.

Prophet Lut

(alayhi as-salaam – peace be upon him)

Lut was Ibrahim's nephew. They were once companions, travelling together and preaching the Word of God, but then Allah summoned Lut to Sodom and the neighbouring city of Gomorrah, situated on the highroad from Makkah to Syria.

Never was any society so morally degraded as Sodom and Gomorrah. Prosperous, yet immoral and corrupt beyond imagination, they openly robbed and killed travellers crossing the outskirts of the cities. Even worse, the men had a greater desire for their own sex, enticing young men to share their beds instead of wives.

Relentlessly, Lut preached to them, urging them to leave their licentious ways, but to no avail. They only jeered at him and insulted him; and despite his warning that Allah would surely punish them, they began to threaten him and his family.

"Bring Allah's punishment if you are telling the truth," they taunted.

Meanwhile, angels visited Ibrahim to inform him of the impending doom of the people of Sodom and Gomorrah. Assuring Ibrahim that Lut and his family would be safe, the angels then set off towards Sodom, arriving outside the city walls late in the afternoon. Lut's daughter happened to be filling her water pitcher nearby; and when she looked up and saw the strangers approaching, she was astonished at their beauty.

"O maiden!" said one of them. "Is there any place in the city where we may find rest?"

Knowing the shameless character of her people, she was afraid to let them enter the city alone, so she asked them to wait while she went to fetch her father. Lut arrived in great haste, fearful for the strangers' safety. He asked them where they had come from and where they were going, but they did not reply. Instead, they asked if they could stay with him. Lut did not know what to say. Of course, he wanted to offer them his hospitality, but it was too risky for them to enter the city in daylight. They would have to wait outside the city walls until nightfall, he told them.

As soon as it was dark, Lut escorted the handsome young strangers to his house. After making them comfortable, he asked his wife to serve them with whatever food they had. Not long after, a mob gathered outside demanding to see his secret guests. But how was that possible? No one apart from his own family saw them enter or knew of their presence, so how did the people find out about them? Mortified, he suddenly realized that his wife must be responsible. She was a troublemaker and had the habit of informing others whenever Lut was entertaining guests. If it were daytime, she would sneak onto the roof and create a smoke to signal that there were guests in the house. If it were night-time, she would light a fire for all to see.

Lut addressed the lecherous mob outside and begged them to go home to their wives and leave his guests alone, but they were determined to have their way. It was men they craved, not women; and someone had informed them that Lut's guests were exceptionally handsome. Completely unruffled by the commotion outside, Lut's guests assured him that no harm would come to them. They were, in fact, angels, sent by Allah to warn him. Before dawn, Lut must leave the city with his family, they told him, and not look back, not even for a moment.

In great haste, Lut's family fled the city, except for his wife who remained behind. Urging everyone forward and onwards from the rear, Lut made sure they did not stop or look back. And not a moment too soon! As they were climbing the hills beyond the two cities of Sodom and Gomorrah, a violent wind swept across the land and stones of baked clay rained down from the sky.

Horrific, deafening wailing and screaming resounded from all directions, but heeding the angels' warning they hurried on their way and did not look back. Now doomed, the two cities were razed to the ground, and everyone perished.

Lut and his family walked on until they reached the safety of Ibrahim's home. From then onwards, they stayed together, preaching Allah's Message.

Author's Comments

On the eastern side of the Dead Sea, where the two cities of Sodom and Gomorrah once stood, is a place covered with sulphurous salts, deadly to animal and plant life. A scene of utter desolation and a warning of the devastation that awaits those who disobey Allah.

Strange human relationships exist in our world. People cohabit without marriage; men marry men; and women marry women. According to Hadith, marriage is half of faith. It is a sacred union between man and woman for the sake of living a pure, wholesome life together and for procreation.

Prophet Yusaf

(alayhi as-salaam – peace be upon him)

Prophet Ibrahim had two sons, Isma'il and Ishaq. Isma'il was his firstborn from his servant wife, Hajarah. Years later, when his first wife, Sarah, was old and had lost all hope of ever having a child, she gave birth to Ishaq (Isaac).

Ishaq grew into a fine young man and married Rebikah (Rebecca) who bore him twin sons, al-Eis (Esau) and Yaqub (Jacob). Although they were twins, the two brothers were very different in looks and disposition and went their separate ways. Al-Eis became the patriarch of the Edomites and the Amalekites. Yaqub became known by the title, Israel, and all his descendants were thereafter known as Bani Israel, the Children of Israel.

Yaqub settled in the land of Canaan (Syria). He married and had six sons and a daughter from his wife, Layya (Leah) and four sons from two other wives. When Layya died, he married her sister, Rahil (Rachel), who bore him two more sons, Yusaf (Joseph) and Benyamin (Benjamin). But soon after giving birth to Benyamin, Rahil died.

Yaqub was extremely fond of his two infant sons; and after their mother's death he took special interest in their upbringing. This made his other sons extremely jealous, especially of Yusaf who was exceptionally beautiful. To protect him, Yaqub entrusted him to his paternal aunt.

Sometime later, he requested her to return Yusaf, but she refused. How could she part with him, she argued? The boy was so young, and she adored him. But then she had a sudden change of heart and agreed to let him go. In fact, she had devised a clever plan that would allow her to keep him for good. Before sending him back to his father, she tied an antique waistband, a legacy from Ishaq, under his clothes.

As soon as she knew Yusaf had reached his father's home, she raised the alarm that the precious waistband had been stolen. It was discovered, of course, on Yusaf; and according to the law she now had the right to keep him as her slave. Her clever ruse had worked. Later, however, the truth became known and Yusaf went back to live with his father.

Yusaf had an engaging personality and was extremely good-looking. Moreover, there was something special about him. One night, he had a strange dream.

"I saw in a dream eleven stars, the sun and the moon, and they all bowed down before me," he told his father.

Yusaf's dream – eleven stars, the sun
and moon bowing down to him.

Being a prophet, Yaqub understood the meaning of the dream; and he knew that one day Yusaf would also be a prophet.

"Don't tell your brothers," he warned him. "They are already jealous of you. They will be even more jealous if you tell them about your dream and might even plot to harm you."

He then explained the meaning of the dream. "My son, Your Lord will choose you as a leader and among other things He will teach you the interpretation of dreams; and He will favour you as He favoured your forefathers, Ishaq and Ibrahim."

Although Yusaf kept the dream a secret from his brothers, they somehow came to know about it. This new revelation made them even more jealous and hostile towards him. They also felt threatened. Was this little brother of theirs really going to become their leader? Would he prove them worthless and deprive them of their inheritance? Even if they ignored the dream, the fact remained that Yusaf was clearly their father's favourite.

"It's not fair," said one of them. "Yusaf and Benyamin are only boys, but they are much dearer to our father than we are. We are older and stronger. He should favour us, not them."

"Yes," the others agreed. "And our father loves Yusaf so much, he cannot bear to let him out of his sight, not even for a moment."

"Let's get rid of him. Let's kill him," one of them suggested, "then our father will favour us instead."

Another brother, fearful of being party to a dreadful crime, put forward a different proposal. "No! Don't kill him," he said. "Let us put him down a well. A caravan of traders will find him when they stop for water and take him along with them. That way, we will be rid of him forever without actually harming him. We will not be blamed."

All the brothers agreed that this was the best plan, so they asked their father if they could take Yusaf with them into the fields.

"Send him with us and let him play and enjoy himself. We promise to take care of him," they said.

Yaqub silently shook his head. "I am afraid that while you are not looking a wolf might attack and kill him," he replied.

Now, Yaqub had genuine cause to be fearful because packs of hungry wolves frequently roamed the wilderness. Moreover, he had recently dreamt that he was standing on the top of a hill looking down on Yusaf who was on the lower slopes. Suddenly, ten wolves surrounded the child and were about to attack him. One of the wolves leapt forward, rescued him, and later released him in a safe place.

"But father," they argued. "We are strong men. We will not let any harm come to him. We promise you."

Reluctantly, and because it was Allah's will, Yaqub agreed. So, the brothers took Yusaf with them the following morning. It was the very first time they were entrusted with him; and it was to be the last. When they reached the fields, they told

Yusaf to remove his shirt. They then lowered him into a dark, dank well and left him. Terrified, Yusaf pleaded with them to pull him out, but the heartless brothers ignored his cries and continued working in the fields until it was time to go home.

"Oh father! Something terrible has happened," they wailed, beating their heads as they entered the house. "While we were racing with one another, a wolf came and devoured Yusaf." And they showed him the shirt, which they had stained with animal blood.

Although deeply grieved, Yaqub had quietly observed that the shirt showed no sign of an attack. It had not the slightest tear. Only the false blood. Also, through divine wisdom, he knew Yusaf was not dead. But for the time being, he was gone, a separation he knew he would find difficult to bear.

"I shall be patient," he said. "Only Allah can save us from your lies."

Meanwhile, in the cold darkness of the well, Yusaf had managed to scramble onto a protruding rock where he sat patiently awaiting his fate. He had stopped crying. No one was around to hear him, and he knew none of his brothers would come to get him out. Instead, he began to pray. Allah comforted him and told him that one day he would remind his brothers of what they did.

Later however, one of the brothers came back to give him food and water. He came again the next day to check whether he was still there and that he was safe. On the third day, a caravan stopped at the well, and as one of them lowered the bucket to draw water he discovered Yusaf. He shouted excitedly to the others and beckoned them to come and help pull him out.

The enthusiasm of the people of the caravan soon dissipated as they deliberated over what to do with their unusual find. The boy was not theirs and someone might question them along the way as to how they came by him. It seems Yusaf may have been too afraid or traumatised by his ordeal to offer any explanation. Whatever their fears, they decided to conceal him among their merchandise and take him along with them. The journey was a long and tedious one; their destination Egypt, a prosperous land but one of idol-worshippers.

When they arrived in Egypt, the caravaners were so eager to be rid of the boy they sold him to the slave trader for just a few silver coins. At the slave market, there was fierce bargaining for the strikingly handsome child. Al-Aziz, Captain of Pharaoh's guard, outbid everyone and was very pleased.

"Make him comfortable," he told his wife, Zulaikah. "He might profit us in some way. We might even adopt him as our son."

And so, they kept him, not as a son, but as a trusted servant.

Yusaf grew into a fine young man, noble, good-natured, and so handsome that Zulaikah fell madly in love with him. She tried desperately to tempt him to love her in return, but Yusaf was a man of supreme moral character. One day, seizing the opportunity to be alone with him, she called him to her room and closed the door to trap him inside.

"Come! Come to me!" she implored, but Yusaf stepped away from her.

"Your husband is my master," he said. "He has always taken care of me. I shall never betray him." And he raced towards the door.

In a desperate bid to stop him, Zulaikah grabbed hold of his shirt. Equally desperate to get away, Yusaf tried to free himself and in the struggle his shirt was torn. He managed to open the door, only to find al-Aziz himself standing there.

"What would be the punishment for a man who tried to seduce your wife?" Zulaikah asked him, trying to cover up her guilt. "Shouldn't he be sent to prison?"

"It was she who tried to tempt me," Yusaf explained. "Look! She has torn my shirt."

A member of the royal household was standing nearby. "Examine Yusaf's shirt," he advised al-Aziz. "If it is torn from the front, your wife is telling the truth, but if it is torn from behind, then she is lying and Yusaf is innocent."

When al-Aziz saw that Yusaf's shirt was, in fact, torn from behind, he told his wife to apologise and seek forgiveness from her gods; and he advised Yusaf not to tell anyone about the incident and to avoid Zulaikah's presence in future.

Word soon reached the wives of the officials close to al-Aziz that his wife was madly in love with her servant. When the malicious rumours spread even further, Zulaikah decided to put an end to them, not only because her honour was at stake, but because Yusaf had rejected her advances. It was customary for servants to obey without question, but hers was a servant with a firm mind and highly principled conscience. She wanted revenge. And she wanted all the women to see why she had risked her honour and reputation. Surely, they would stop blaming her when they saw how irresistibly handsome her servant was.

She invited all the women to a sumptuous banquet and gave each of them a knife to cut the food. When they were busy, chatting, and slicing fruit, she called Yusaf into the banquet hall. Stunned by his beauty, the women could not take their eyes off him and accidentally cut their hands.

"Oh, this cannot be a mortal!" they exclaimed. "This must surely be a noble angel."

"Now do you understand why I wanted him to love me?" Zulaikah said. "And if he still resists, I will make sure he goes to prison."

Yusaf overheard what she said. "O my Lord!" he prayed. "I would rather go to prison than commit such a sin. Please save me from their evil plot."

The women backed Zulaikah and tried to coerce Yusaf into obeying her, but he remained steadfast. So, they all swore before the king that Yusaf had seduced the wife of al-Aziz; and just as Zulaikah had planned, Yusaf was sent to prison. Although he suspected Yusaf was innocent, the king deemed it wise to have him locked away for a while to allow the slanderous gossip to die down, but as time passed, he forgot about him.

In the prison, Yusaf shared a cell with two of the palace servants accused of plotting to poison the king, their cases still pending investigation. One was the royal cupbearer who used to prepare the king's drinks. The other was the palace baker. Recently, both prisoners had seen strange dreams and they asked Yusaf if he could interpret them.

"I dreamt that I was pressing grapes to make wine," the cupbearer told Yusaf.

"In my dream, I was carrying a basket of bread on my head and the birds were eating it," said the baker.

"I shall tell you the interpretation of your dreams for my Lord has taught me how, but first I must tell you that I have forsaken the religion of those who disbelieve in Allah and the Hereafter. I follow the religion of my father, Yaqub, and my forefathers, Ishaq and Ibrahim. My fellow prisoners, those whom you worship besides Allah are only names you and your fathers have invented. Allah commands you to worship none but Him. This is the right way.

"As for your dreams, one of you will be set free and will again pour wine for the king. The other will be crucified and the birds will peck at his head. This is the interpretation of your dreams," he explained.

"Please mention me to your master so that I may also be freed," he said to royal cupbearer, but the man forgot and Yusaf remained in prison.

One night, the king had a strange dream. Baffled, and curious to know the meaning of the dream, he called his ministers.

"I saw in my dream seven fat cows being devoured by seven lean cows; and I saw seven green ears of corn and seven golden, dry ones. Now tell me the meaning of my dream."

His ministers shook their heads. "Sounds like muddled fantasies. We are not skilled in the interpretation of dreams," they apologetically replied.

Standing nearby was the royal cupbearer who had been in prison with Yusaf. "I can tell you the meaning of your dream," he said, suddenly remembering his cellmate. "Just grant me permission to visit the prison."

"O Yusaf, man of truth! Explain this dream that I may inform the king," said the cup-bearer, and he related the king's strange dream.

"For seven years you shall sow the corn seeds as usual, but when you reap each harvest use only a little of the corn. The rest you must store away. After the seven years of abundance, there will be seven years of famine when you will almost finish the corn you have stored. Then will come a year of abundant rainfall, and the people will press seeds for oil and grapes for wine."

When the cupbearer conveyed Yusaf's interpretation of the dream, the king commanded him to fetch him immediately. Yusaf, of course, longed to be free, but he wanted first to clear himself of the false charges made by Zulaikah and her women friends. He also wanted al-Aziz to know that he had never betrayed his trust.

"Return to your master," he told the cupbearer, "and ask him about the women who cut their hands?"

The king immediately understood and called Zulaikah and her friends to ask them the truth about the affair.

"Yusaf is innocent," admitted Zulaikah. "I am the one to blame."

Yusaf was then set free and brought before the king who asked him again about his dream. Yusaf repeated the interpretation and revealed further details the king had not mentioned to anyone. Realising that here was a man of exceptional qualities, the king declared, "From this day, you shall have a position of high rank; one where you are fully trusted."

"Then set me in charge of all the storehouses of the land," Yusaf requested, "and I will manage them honestly and prudently."

So, he gave Yusaf an honoured position, the second highest in the land. And just as Yusaf had foretold, there were seven years of abundance during which time he worked tirelessly to keep the granaries and storehouses of Egypt well-stocked.

During the seven years of famine that followed, people flocked to the city to buy grain. One day, his brothers were among them. Yusaf recognized them immediately, but they did not recognize him. How could they? He was just a boy of about seven years old when they lowered him into the well. Now, he was fully-grown and the second most powerful man in Egypt.

When they had received their grain, Yusaf called them and asked them to bring their youngest brother with them next time so that he could give them an extra measure of corn. He warned them that if they did not bring him, they would not receive any corn at all. Meanwhile, he had instructed his servants to put the money and merchandise his brothers had given in exchange for corn back into their bags. Having money and goods with which to barter would ensure they would come for corn again, bringing Benyamin with them.

Back home, Yaqub was eagerly awaiting his sons' return. When they came and told him that next time they must take Benyamin with them, he was deeply troubled. Benyamin was a comfort and pleasure to him in his old age. How could he let him go so far from home? And how could he trust his sons when they had deceived him long ago by taking Yusaf from him? However, there were many mouths to feed. The corn would not last long. And as Yusaf had planned, the discovery of the money and goods in their bags made it easy for his brothers to return. Making his sons first swear a solemn oath that they would bring Benyamin safely back home, Yaqub finally agreed to let him go with them.

Overjoyed to see his younger brother after so many years, Yusaf took him aside and told him who he was. He also confided in him his secret plan to bring all his family to live with him in Egypt. When his brothers' sacks had been filled with corn, he ordered a servant to place the king's drinking cup in Benyamin's sack.

Just as they were leaving, the city's Crier raised an alarm. "Hey! You in the caravan! You are thieves."

"What has been stolen?" they asked.

"The king's drinking cup," the Crier replied. "Whoever returns it will be given a camel load of corn as a reward."

"By Allah! We are not thieves," the brothers insisted. "We came here to buy corn, not to create mischief."

"If it is proved that you are liars, then what should be the penalty?" the Crier asked.

"The person in whose sack the cup is found should be severely punished," they replied.

The Crier then led them back to Yusaf who ordered his servants to search their sacks. The brothers were horrified when the king's drinking cup was found in Benyamin's sack.

"Small wonder!" they blurted out. "His brother was also a thief."

They were, of course, referring to the fabricated incident of the missing waistband. But knowing it had been a lie, they hastily changed tact and appealed to the minister's good nature instead.

"O ruler of this land! Our father is an old man and will grieve terribly the loss of his youngest son. Take one of us in his place," they begged. "Surely, you are generous and kind and will listen to our plea."

Yusaf, however, was firm. "By Allah! How can we punish anyone but the one in whose sack the cup was found?"

The eldest brother, Ruebel, stood resolutely beside Benyamin. "I will not leave this land until my father gives me permission or until Benyamin is released," he told his brothers. "So go home, and tell our father what has happened, and ask the other people in our caravan to bear witness that what you tell him is true."

When he received this dreadful news, Yaqub was so overwhelmed with grief that he lost his sight.

"By Allah!" the brothers lamented. "You will never stop remembering Yusaf until your health is ruined."

"I reveal my anguish and grief only to Allah," he told them. "And Allah has given me knowledge about things you know nothing about. So go! Find out about Yusaf and his brother Benyamin."

"O ruler of this land!" the brothers said to Yusaf. "Hard times have hit our family. We have little to barter with. Please be charitable and give us full measure of corn. Truly, Allah rewards the generous and charitable."

"Do you remember what you did with your brother, Yusaf?" he asked them.

The brothers stared at him, shocked, and utterly confused. How did he know they had a brother named Yusaf? They had never mentioned his name. Memories of Yusaf raced through their minds, and they began to wonder if this man could be the brother whom they had rid themselves of so many years ago. As emotions swayed between astonishment, guilt, and fear, they finally dared to ask, "Are you Yusaf?"

"Yes, I am indeed your brother, Yusaf," he replied. "Allah has truly blessed me. And Allah surely rewards those who fear and obey Him, and those who are patient."

Ashamed and truly penitent, the brothers wondered if Yusaf could ever forgive them for what they had done to him.

"You are forgiven," Yusaf assured them. "Now, take my shirt. Lay it on my father's face and his sight will be restored. Then bring him to me. Bring all your family."

So, in great haste, the brothers set off to tell their father the good news. They were still a long way from home when Yaqub told his other sons that he could smell Yusaf's shirt.

"By God!" they said. "You will not cease to remember Yusaf until you are a dotard or death overcomes you."

On their arrival, the brothers did what Yusaf had told them and Yaqub regained his sight. His patience finally rewarded, all that remained was to be reunited with his beloved son. And now that the truth was out in the open, the brothers asked their father to pray for their forgiveness.

And so they came, all of them, to Egypt. And despite all the trials and heartache he had endured, Yusaf harboured no bitterness. He felt only love for his family, and gratitude to Almighty Allah for reuniting him with them.

When everyone bowed down before Yusaf, he turned to his father and said, "Do you remember, father? This is what I dreamt when I was a boy."

Author's Comments

Most parents love all their children equally, but sometimes they pay more attention to one child because they have special needs or because Allah has gifted them with special qualities. Yusaf received special attention from his father, not because of his good looks or because he lost his mother at a tender age, but because, through divine knowledge, Yaqub knew he was destined for a special role in life – that of a prophet.

Yaqub was an exceptionally devoted father who loved all his children, not only when they were good, but unconditionally, regardless of how they behaved. He knew his older sons lied about Yusaf's tragic misadventure, but he did not punish them, nor did he speak harshly to them. Likewise, children should love and respect their parents, especially when they are old, regardless of their behaviour towards them. In the Qur'an Allah says, "Respect your parents." He does not say, "Respect them only if they are good to you."

Similarly, we should love our children, not conditionally, when or because they are good, but because they need our love. Love nurtures goodness, just as Yaqub's love for his sons softened their hearts and instilled feelings of shame and repentance when they were finally re-united with Yusaf.

Although Yusaf underwent great trials and hardships, he remained steadfast throughout and harboured no bitterness in his heart. Yusaf's story also exemplifies the virtue of patience. Both Yusaf and Yaqub, inspired by their complete faith in Allah, had infinite patience as well as generous, compassionate hearts and a forgiving nature.

This story also highlights the sublime virtue of resisting temptation; and it warns us against jealousy. The first sin committed in Paradise was due to Iblis's jealousy of Adam; that Allah had created him the best of His creation. And the first murder committed by humanity was the result of Qabil's jealousy of his brother, Habil. Similarly, it was jealousy that incited Yusaf's brothers to devise their evil plot to be rid of him. So beware! Jealousy eats away at the goodness in a person's heart and can turn him into a fiend.

Finally, the story of Yusaf teaches us that truth prevails, and that patience and goodness are amply rewarded.

Prophet Ayyub

(alayhi as-salaam – peace be upon him)

A descendent of Prophet Ibrahim, through his son, Ishaq (Isaac), Ayyub was the epitome of righteousness and Patience personified. Forever generous and good-hearted, he showed profound respect for his parents, gave food and water to the poor and needy, and shelter to the orphans. He treated his servants kindly and went out of his way to help those who were weak and oppressed, and to defend the wrongly accused. He was also extremely wealthy, possessing land as well as livestock.

Ayyub, like all prophets, devoted his life to the worship of Allah and was forever grateful for His blessings. The more he worshipped, the more prosperous he became; and the more prosperous he became, the greater his desire to please Allah by helping those in need. Every waking hour he preached, warning his people about the consequences of disobedience, disbelief, and sinfulness.

People could not understand why his prosperity did not distract him from his worship. They accused him of worshipping Allah only to keep his wealth; and rumours spread that if he became poor, he would forget Allah. Of course, Ayyub, ignored their wicked rumours, but to test him and prove the disbelievers wrong, Allah drastically reversed his fortune. He lost all his wealth and his health deteriorated so much that he could barely stand.

The spiteful gossip continued with fluctuating ambience. Some said he was not a prophet after all and only pretended to worship Allah. Some argued that if he was indeed a prophet, he deserved better treatment and Allah should put an end to his suffering. Others delighted in his misfortune and claimed Allah was punishing him to satisfy his enemies. All predicted Ayyub would lose heart and leave his faith.

They were wrong. Despite all his hardships, he continued to worship Allah. His patience seemed limitless, and his faith was even stronger than when he had enjoyed good health and prosperity. The few who believed in him were full of admiration and prayed for him, earnestly requesting Allah to reward him by restoring all that he had lost. But Ayyub's troubles were not yet over; and the devil was determined to bring about his downfall.

Seven long years passed, and his illness worsened. He became weak and pale. His skin began to rot, emitting an unbearable odour, forcing his friends, his children, and even his parents to abandon him. Only his loyal, caring wife, Layya, stayed.

She tried to ignore the evil gossip, but the devil does not give up easily. Doubts and confusion unsettled her mind, and she began to question her husband.

"Why has Allah inflicted you with such hardship? Where has your youth, your health and wealth gone? And where are all your friends and family?" she asked.

"Be careful, my wife! The devil is trying to undermine your faith," Ayyub warned her.

"We have suffered long enough," Layya persisted. "Why don't you ask your God to relieve you of all your troubles?"

Ayyub looked sternly at her and asked, "How long did we enjoy an easy life?"

"Forty years," she answered.

"And how long have we suffered hardship?"

"Seven years," she said.

"Then shame on you to suggest that I ask Allah to relieve me of my suffering," Ayyub scolded. "I am appalled by what you say and utterly disappointed in you. If you are no longer content with the Will of Allah it means your faith is weak."

Suddenly, he lost his temper and cursed her. "I swear I will thrash you a hundred times. Go! Leave me alone!"

Ayyub praying after all his family and
friends had abandoned him.

Layya's mind was in turmoil; and although it troubled her to go, she left him to endure all his pain and suffering alone.

Ayyub, however, had never doubted that Allah was watching over him. Never for a moment had his faith faltered. His wife's lack of faith had made him extremely angry, but he had never been angry with God.

Silently, fervently, he prayed, "O Allah! Distress has seized me, but You are the Most Merciful of the Merciful."

Allah ordered Ayyub to strike the ground with his feet, and miraculously a spring gushed forth, providing fresh water for him to drink and to bathe his rotting flesh. Thereafter, his health and strength returned, and he felt better than he had ever felt before. Allah had finally put an end to all his hardship.

"We answered him, removed his suffering and restored his family to him ... as an act of grace from Us and a reminder for all who worship Us." Holy Qur'an, 21: 84.

After deserting him, Layya became so miserable she decided to go back and care for him again, but she couldn't find him anywhere. Still searching, she came across a strong, healthy young man she had never met before, or so she thought.

"A sick old man used to live here. Have you seen him? Do you know where he is?" she asked.

"Has your eyesight become so weak that you cannot see who is standing before you?" he replied.

The voice was all too familiar. Could this be her husband, she wondered? When she realised it was indeed Ayyub, she was overjoyed. Thanking Allah for His blessings, she also prayed for forgiveness.

Ayyub suddenly remembered the oath, to strike his wife a hundred lashes. In those days, oaths were strictly adhered to, but Allah knew Ayyub had spoken in anger and had not intended to cause Layya harm, so He commanded him to take a bundle of thin grass and strike her with them, thus fulfilling the oath.

Ayyub's entire family returned to live with him, and Allah blessed him with more children and even greater prosperity than before. A noble Messenger, he spent the rest of his life praying and preaching the Word of God.

Author's Comments

Patience is a virtue only true believers possess. Besides having complete faith in Allah, the believers know that difficulties and disappointments in life are often blessings in disguise. It is also Allah's way of testing, guiding, and moulding us to strengthen and perfect us, that we may be hopeful of His ultimate mercy and a place in Paradise.

"Do you think you will enter Paradise before Allah has tested you? ... You shall certainly be tested with your wealth and yourself." Holy Qur'an, 3: 142, 186.

"Moreover, the believers know that only Allah can lighten their burden, for He is the One Who sent it in order to test them; and they also know that Allah does not impose on anyone more than they can bear." Holy Qur'an, 2: 286.

Ayyub's wife was guilty of a common human failing. She focused on her present situation and forgot all the good times, all the blessings she had enjoyed. All too often, when someone does something wrong, we tend to focus our attention on that one wrong, forgetting all the kindness and the times he or she lent a helping hand.

People tried their utmost to shake Ayyub's faith but failed. Like all prophets, Ayyub had one aim, to serve and please Allah. Most people try to please others, but it is not easy to please them. In fact, it is virtually impossible. All too often, whatever we do makes no difference; they still complain.

It helps to remember a simple rule: always try to please Allah because if Allah is pleased with us then good people will also be pleased. Trying to please sinful or foolish people is futile. There is no pleasing them however hard we try. The devil is on their side; and the devil is the Great Complainer. Never happy, never satisfied!

Prophet Shuaib

(alayhi as-salaam – peace be upon him)

Prophet Shuaib was given the momentous task of reforming the people of Madyan. Although a wandering tribe, their main settlement was in the north-east Sinai Peninsula on the commercial highway between Egypt and the Mesopotamian empires of Assyria and Babylon. They were also known as Companions of the Woods or Ashab-al-Aykah because, among other deities, they worshipped a large tree called Aykah.

They were commercial traders by profession, enjoying prosperity and comfortable living, but their affluence was the result of fraudulent dealings. They gave less weight and short measure, hid any defects in their goods, and charged more than they were worth. They would trim the edges of gold and silver coins and then channel them at par value back into circulation; this practice being the main source of their wealth. But worse still, they were guilty of the major sins: disbelief in Allah and the worship of false gods.

Shuaib, who was well known for his eloquence, begged them to leave their wicked ways and to be mindful of Allah's blessings, lest He take away their comforts and reverse their good fortune. But sadly, his words fell on deaf ears.

"We do not understand what you say, or what you demand of us," they mockingly replied. "All we see is a weak man and were it not for the fact that you belong to a noble family we would certainly have stoned you to death."

"O my people! Do you consider my family to be more important than Allah?" Shuaib patiently replied. "You may have turned your backs on Him, but beware! He sees everything you do."

So fervent was his desire to reform them for their own good, he spent hours weeping and praying for them. Some say he wept so much that he became blind, and that when Allah restored his sight, he continued his mission with even deeper compassion and concern for them. Repeatedly, earnestly, he assured them he only wanted to guide them for their own sake, not for any personal gain, but to no avail. Oblivious of the consequences, they continued to treat him with conceit and contempt.

"You are possessed. And you are a liar. But if you are telling the truth then prove it. Make a piece of the sky fall down on us."

Unremittingly, they hurled sarcastic remarks at him. "You are a tolerant, sensible man of wisdom. Does your prayer command you that we should abandon what our forefathers worshipped? And does it restrict us from doing whatever we please with our own property?"

Shuaib tried to convince them that whatever he was doing was according to Allah's command and was for their own good. He also warned them that to disbelieve in him and his Message might result in a disastrous fate like the peoples of Nuh, Hud and Salih. But as always, they resented his advice. Worse still, they unanimously resolved to be rid of him. So, they set upon him and his followers and drove them out of the city. It was a blessing in disguise because the people of Madyan were now doomed.

Days of scorching heat were followed by ominous gloom and eerie stillness. Huge black clouds loomed overhead, but they did not release the cooling rain they so desperately needed. Instead, it rained down fire. The sky had indeed fallen on them.

A violent earthquake followed, destroying everything in the land. All perished, except Shuaib and his band of faithful followers.

Author's Comments

No one likes to be cheated. If we are honest and fair in all our dealings, personal, social, and commercial, we can hope to earn Allah's pleasure and avoid His wrath. The people of Madyan were not driven to unscrupulous ways by poverty or necessity, but by greed. They were corrupt by choice. In addition to fraudulent dealings, they were guilty of two major sins, khufr and shirk – disbelief in Allah and the worship of false gods.

It is also evident from their response to Shuaib's pleadings that they did not understand the true purpose of religion. To them, it simply comprised the worship of their so-called gods. In no way did it relate to how they behaved in their daily lives. How unfortunate for them that they did not follow their own noble Messenger's example. And how fortunate for us that we have Islam to guide us; its teachings encompassing all aspects of our lives, physical, material, social, as well as spiritual.

Prophet Musa

(alayhi as-salaam – peace be upon him)

Prophet Yaqub (Jacob) and all his family settled in the land of Egypt. Yaqub was also known by the name Israel, and the families of his twelve sons were known as the tribes of Bani Israel Children of Israel. Clever and industrious by nature, they adapted well to life in their newly adopted land and became prosperous.

But then there came to the throne of Egypt an arrogant, ruthless Pharaoh named Ramesis, also known as Firaun. Alongside their idols, the Egyptians worshipped Firaun like a god, and all bowed down before him. Except the Israelites! And for their refusal to comply, Firaun utterly despised them and relentlessly, mercilessly persecuted them. But no amount of suffering or hardship would force them to abandon their God and bow down to him.

One night, Firaun dreamt that a baby boy born to the Israelites would one day usurp his throne and destroy his empire. Thereafter, his hatred for them intensified. He also began to fear them. The only way to protect himself and his kingdom, he decided, would be to kill every baby boy born to Bani Israel.

Under cover of darkness, the cruel massacre began. The spine-chilling cries of women desperately pleading, screaming hysterically, echoed through the night; and the pungent smell of fresh blood hung in the air as soldiers charged into the houses, snatched the babies from their mother's arms or from the cribs, killing every baby boy, sparing only the girls.

Yukabid cleverly hid her baby son, Musa, in her home for as long as she could, but lived in constant fear that soldiers might one day discover him and kill him. Early one morning, guided by divine inspiration, she wrapped him in a blanket and placed him in a wooden casket. Gently, and cautiously, looking around to be sure no one was watching, she set the casket down on the River Nile. Although Allah had assured her that He would return Musa to her, it must not have been easy, letting her precious baby go and watch him drift slowly downstream, further, and further away.

She told her daughter, Miriam, to follow the casket and watch where it went. So, treading quietly in the water at the river's edge, hidden by the long reeds, the little girl followed as it drifted along. Bobbing gently with the current, it entered a stream that flowed through Firaun's garden. There, one of the maidservants spotted it and brought it to Firaun's wife, Asiyah. The moment Asiyah set eyes on the beautiful baby boy, she wanted to keep him.

Discovery of baby Musa; the parting of the
sea; and Musa receiving the tablets.

"Please don't kill him. The river has brought him to us, so maybe he will bring us luck. Let us keep him and adopt him as our son." And because it was Allah's plan, Firaun agreed.

Still hidden among the reeds, Miriam was watching, listening, and waiting. When baby Musa began to cry unconsolably, Asiyah ordered her maidservant to find a woman to wet-nurse him. Miriam immediately rushed forward.

"Shall I fetch a woman who will nurse him and care for him?" she said.

Asiyah agreed, and Miriam raced home to tell her mother the good news. Yukabid was so ecstatic, she almost blurted out the truth that the baby was hers, but Allah helped her to control her tongue and gave her the strength and patience to keep her secret. And that is how baby Musa miraculously survived the terrible persecution.

Years passed, and Musa grew into a handsome young man. As Firaun's adopted son, he was familiar with the Egyptian way of life and their worship of animal gods. The dog Anubis, so-called custodian of the dead; Apis the sacred bull; Ibis, the bird god of wisdom and magic; and other gods that represented natural forces. And there was Firaun, the self-acclaimed god of them all.

Musa was honest, good-hearted, and much admired. He was intelligent and wise, and because his own birth mother had nursed him, he fully understood the sentiments of his own people. Most importantly, Allah had chosen him to be a noble Messenger. His first mission would be to spread the religion of the One True God, his second, to free the Israelites from Egyptian bondage!

Musa would often leave the palace secretly and mingle with the people in the city. He saw how the elite, the ruling class, lived in luxury while the rest lived as slaves; how the Israelites lived in bondage, forced to do all manner of menial and strenuous tasks; and how the Egyptians despised and ill-treated them. He had come to know the truth about himself, that he was an Israelite by birth, so what he saw deeply troubled him.

One day, he was passing through the Israelite settlement when he saw an Egyptian brutally attacking a man. He immediately intervened and struck the Egyptian a blow so forceful it killed him instantly. Musa was horrified. He only hit the man to warn him not to treat an Israelite in this way. It had never been his intention to kill or seriously harm him.

Overcome with remorse, he prayed, "O my Lord! Forgive me, for I have done a terrible thing. Never again will I help the mischief makers."

Musa moved stealthily about the city, nervously looking out for enemies, afraid that someone would recognise him. Strange as it may seem, the very next day, he came across the same Israelite who had caused him to commit the terrible crime, and he was again in trouble. Musa's immediate thought was that this man must be a troublemaker. When he questioned him, however, he realised that once again the

Egyptian was to blame. He was about to confront him when the Egyptian cautioned him.

"Do you intend to kill me as you killed a man yesterday? Then your aim is only to become a troublemaker and not a righteous person."

At that very moment, a man came running to him. "O Musa!" he cried. "The chiefs are holding council about you, to decide whether to kill you or not. So, take my advice and escape while you can."

News of the killing had indeed reached Firaun. The palace was no longer safe. No place was safe. Concealed by his long cloak, Musa stealthily left the city, not knowing where he was going or what he was going to do. He prayed for protection from the wrongdoers and asked God to guide him to the right way.

He arrived at a well in Madyan (Midian) where a group of men were watering their herd of livestock. Standing nearby, two young maidens were struggling to control their thirsty animals. Musa asked them why they were holding them back.

"We cannot water them until the men move on," one of them explained. "Our father is a very old man, so we have to look after the herd."

Musa helped them water their animals and then watched as they set off back home. Sad, weary and forlorn, he sat down in the shade of a tree to rest. "My Lord!" he prayed. "Truly, I am in need of whatever good You may bestow upon me."

Soon after, one of the maidens came to him. "My father calls you," she said. "He wants to reward you for watering our animals." And she led the way to her house.

Musa related his story to the old man whose name was Shuaib. "Don't be afraid," Shuaib assured him. "You have escaped from the mischief-makers."

"Why don't you hire him," suggested one of his daughters. "He is young and strong and seems trustworthy."

Shuaib appreciated her idea, but he had a better one. "Marry one of my daughters and in return you must serve me for eight years. If you wish, you may serve me for ten years, but that is up to you. I do not wish to impose any hardship on you. And if Allah wills, you will find me a kind, honest master." So Musa agreed.

When the eight years of the contract were over, he set off with his family to start a new life elsewhere. Along the way, he spotted a fire in the direction of a mountain called Mount Tur (Mount Sinai).

"Wait here!" he told his wife. "I saw a fire in the distance. I might find something there. Or maybe I could bring a piece of burning wood to light a fire to keep you warm." So, she waited with the children while he went to investigate.

The fire was, in fact, a burning bush, and as Musa got closer, he heard a voice call his name.

"O Musa! Truly, I am your Lord! Take off your shoes for you are on sacred ground. I have chosen you, so listen to what I am about to reveal to you. I am Allah, the Lord of all mankind and jinn. None has the right to be worshipped but Me. Worship Me alone and offer prayers."

Musa was so stunned; he stumbled and almost fell to the ground. But then Allah spoke again.

"What is in your right hand, Musa?"

"This is my staff, which I lean on sometimes. I also use it to beat down branches of leaves for my sheep, among other uses," Musa replied.

"Cast it down, Musa!" Allah commanded.

Instantly, the staff began to move along the ground as if it were a serpent. Startled, Musa darted away from it, but Allah called him back.

"O Musa! Draw near and do not be afraid. Take hold of it and it will be as it was. Now put your right hand inside your cloak and then draw it out. It will become dazzling white, not with disease, but with an illuminating light. Then put it back and it will be as it was."

"These are two signs," explained Allah, "miracles from your Lord to Firaun and his chiefs, the wicked disbelievers. Go to Firaun! He has transgressed all limits of disobedience and has behaved as an arrogant tyrant."

"But my Lord," said Musa. "I have killed a man from among them and I fear they may punish me. Bestow me with confidence and boldness and make my task easy for me. Loosen the knot in my tongue that they may understand what I say, and send my brother, Harun (Aaron), with me. He is eloquent and will be my helper and confirm whatever I say. Otherwise, I fear they may not believe me."

When Musa asked Allah to loosen the knot in his tongue, he was referring to a speech defect caused when he was a child. Not realising the danger, he once picked up a burning stick and put it in his mouth, badly burning his tongue.

"We shall strengthen you with your brother," said Allah, "and give power to both of you so they will not be able to harm you. And you will be victorious. Go now to Firaun! Speak to him politely then maybe he will accept My Message. Say you are My Messengers and tell him not to torment the Children of Israel but set them free to go with you."

Musa, accompanied by his brother Harun, thus went to Firaun, and told him about the religion of the One True God, Allah.

"O Firaun!" he said. "I am truly a Messenger from the Lord of all mankind and jinn and all that exists on the earth."

Firaun was truly baffled by this strange apotheosis. A Messenger of the Lord! What Lord, he questioned? And had Musa forgotten that he had brought him up in the palace where all were bound to serve and worship him?

"Tell me about this God you claim is the Lord of all that exists," he mocked.

"He is the Lord of the heavens and the earth and all that is between them," Musa replied.

Firaun sneered and turned to his ministers, Haman and Qarun. "Do you hear what he says?"

"Truly, my Lord is your Lord," said Musa, "and the Lord of your fathers and ancestors."

Smirking conceitedly, Firaun addressed the people. "Truly, this Messenger of yours is a madman."

Undeterred by Firaun's mockery, Musa continued. "He is the Lord of the east and the west and all that is between them, if you could but understand."

Firaun was beginning to lose patience. "If any one of you chooses a god other than me, I will throw you into prison," he threatened.

"I come to you with clear proof," insisted Musa. "So set the people of Israel free."

"Proof?" Firaun questioned, his eyebrows raised and temples throbbing with rage. "What proof? Show me!"

Musa threw down his staff and it became a serpent. He then drew his right hand from inside his robe and it was radiant white.

"He is indeed a clever sorcerer," scoffed Firaun. "What do you think?" he asked his ministers.

"Perhaps he is planning to depose you and take over the land," they replied.

Firaun then turned and stared at Musa. "Did we not bring you up as a child?" he said. "And you lived with us many years until you killed a man. Then you fled in fear."

"Yes, that is true," Musa replied. "But I was ignorant then of Allah's Message. My Lord has since enlightened me with His Knowledge and made me one of His Messengers."

Firaun, now noticeably agitated, consulted with his ministers who advised him to call the best sorcerers in the land to compete with Musa and thus humiliate and defeat him publicly.

On the day of the competition, a huge crowd gathered, excited and eager to watch the spectacle of magic. The sorcerers arrived, full of confidence and assured of a generous reward should they win, as well as high positions in Firaun's court.

"By the might of Firaun, we shall certainly win," they said. "Shall we throw first or will you, Musa?"

"You throw first," said Musa.

So, they threw down their staffs and ropes, which appeared to move fast. The spectators were still loudly applauding when Allah told Musa to throw his staff. Instantly, it turned into a serpent and swallowed up all that the sorcerers had conjured. And when Musa took hold of the serpent it became a staff again.

The sorcerers were astonished. They knew very well that what they did was only trickery, so they had no doubt that Musa had performed a feat far beyond the powers of any sorcerer. Believing this miracle to be a sign from Allah, they fell in prostration.

"We believe in the Lord of Musa and Harun, the Lord of all mankind and jinn," they declared.

Firaun exploded with rage. "You have believed in Musa's Lord before I have given you permission. This is a plot to drive everyone out of the city. As punishment I will cut off your hands and feet from opposite sides and crucify you."

This was no empty threat. Firaun was capable of the most diabolical punishments, especially for those who opposed his authority. But the sorcerers showed no fear.

"You take revenge only because we believe in Allah. If we die, then certainly we are returning to our Lord."

Firaun was now confused. And he felt threatened. No one had ever dared to challenge him like this. "O my people!" he shouted so all could hear. "Am I not the supreme ruler of Egypt and of the rivers flowing at my feet? Am I not better than Musa, this despicable man who can barely express himself? And if he really is a Messenger from his Lord, why has he not been given gold bracelets and angels to protect him?"

With these words, Firaun managed to convince the people and win back their favour. His troubles, however, were far from over. While the magic contest was in progress, Asiyah had kept herself informed of the developments and when she learned that Musa had emerged triumphant, she openly declared that his was the true faith. Disguised, she had mingled with the Israelites and seen how they suffered at the hands of Firaun's men. As hatred for her husband grew, increasing love for the One True God had filled her heart.

The news of his wife's defection struck Firaun like a thunderbolt. Mad with rage, he had her arrested, tried and condemned to death. As she was about to die, she lifted her hands and prayed: "My God! Build for me a house near You in Paradise and save me from Pharaoh and from the wrongdoers."

Musa continued to preach, and Firaun, as before, openly mocked him. "I know of no other god than me, but light the kiln to bake clay bricks," he ordered Haman, "and build a lofty tower that I may stand nearer to heaven and look for the god of Musa, even though I am sure he is a liar."

The use of baked bricks would ensure the foundations and walls could support such a towering edifice. But was the tower built? Or was this merely Firaun's way of ridiculing Musa for daring to suggest there was any deity higher than he? Historical narrations record that Haman did undertake the construction of a lofty building, which collapsed under its own weight before its completion. Only Allah knows.

Firaun was not Musa's only adversary. One of his own people, an Israelite named Qarun, despite knowing the Taurat (Torah) by heart and being an authority on it, persistently challenged Musa and openly defied his teachings. By dint of his God-given talents, Qarun had amassed enormous wealth and power. He had so many chests full of treasures that the keys to unlock them were too heavy for any man to lift. With an air of pomposity, his head held high, and his long robes trailing behind him, he was often seen dragging the hefty chain of keys along the ground.

Qarun's colossal wealth had raised him to a position of high esteem, especially in Firaun's court; and taking clever advantage of this close connection, Firaun used him to spy on the Bani Israel and keep him informed of their activities. Arrogant and boastful, Qarun was an absolute hypocrite, and not only a thorn in Musa's side, but a constant threat to his mission.

Many people envied Qarun for his immense wealth and wished to be like him even though he was not a good man, nor a contented one. He was exceedingly jealous of Musa and Harun. The brothers had no wealth, no worldly treasures to show off, so why had Allah chosen them to lead Bani Israel? Why not him? He had wealth and power as well as connections in high places. Allah should have chosen him instead.

Musa explained that it was Allah's will and that he should accept it, just as he should accept and acknowledge that his worldly gains were all due to Allah's blessings. Musa also encouraged him to give Zakat and to share his wealth for the benefit of others in the hope of earning reward from Allah.

Qarun, however, was excessively greedy and miserly, and nothing could ever persuade him to part with his treasures. His wealth had nothing to do with Allah, he argued. It was the result of his own effort and ingenuity. And because of his pride, ingratitude and miserliness, Allah caused the ground to open beneath him and swallow him up, along with his home and all his treasures.

***

While Firaun remained his usual self, pompous, ruthless, and conceited, his ministers were becoming increasingly agitated.

"Will you leave Musa and his people free to create mischief in the land?" they asked.

"I will not!" Firaun curtly replied. "I will command my soldiers to kill them all. Except Musa! Leave him to me. I will kill him with my own sword and let him call upon his Lord to prevent me."

As word of Firaun's pernicious plan began to spread, Musa urged his people to be patient and pray for Allah's help. "Truly, the earth belongs to Allah. He gives it as heritage to whomever He wills. It may be that your Lord will destroy your enemy and make you successors on the earth."

Fearing persecution from Firaun and his soldiers, many of Musa's own people left him. However, a man in Firaun's own household secretly believed in Musa and tried to warn Firaun.

"Would you kill a man because he claims that Allah is his Lord, even when he has come to you with clear signs? If he is a liar, then upon him will be the sin of his lies, but if he is telling the truth, then the calamities he threatens may well befall you."

Musa also warned Firaun that if he and his people did not obey his Lord, they would be plagued by disasters. And plagued they were! Years of drought and famine followed, but still Firaun and his people refused to believe. Sometimes, they ascribed their calamities to evil omens. Sometimes, they blamed Musa.

"O Musa!" they said. "Whatever message you may bring and whatever magic you may work on us, we will never believe in you and your God."

A succession of disasters followed – the flood, the swarm of locusts, the plague of itching lice, the plague of frogs, and the water turning into blood. Although these were obvious signs of Allah's wrath, they remained firm in their disbelief.

When faced with calamity they would say, "O Musa! If you ask your Lord to remove this punishment, we shall indeed believe in you and set the children of Israel free."

As soon as Allah revoked the punishment, they went back on their words. Allah then took retribution from them by destroying all their grand buildings and works of art. Finally, Allah commanded Musa to lead the tribe of Bani Israel out of the land of Egypt.

"Leave at night," Allah told him, "for the moment he knows you have fled, Firaun and his soldiers will surely pursue you."

Stealthily, in the shadow of night, they began the perilous journey towards the Sinai Peninsula, fear gripping them every step of the way. They knew Firaun well. It would not take him long to discover they were gone, so they had to keep going. No stopping, no looking back, not even for a moment.

All too soon, the deafening sound of galloping horses shattered the quiet of the night; Firaun and his soldiers, getting closer and closer. Desperate and terrified, the Bani Israel struggled on until they reached the Red Sea, but Firaun and his men were hot on their heels. They were trapped. Ahead the mighty sea; behind them, Firaun and his mighty men.

In that moment of panic and despair, Musa also felt helpless, but Allah then commanded him to strike the water with his staff. Immediately, the sea parted and rose as high as mountains with a path of dry land between. With Musa leading, the Bani Israel hurried along as fast as their weary legs could carry them.

As the last of them scrambled safely onto the shore, Firaun and his men finally caught up with them. In chariots and on horseback, they plunged forward, determined to annihilate them all. But Allah had other plans. The mountains of sea suddenly came crashing down on Firaun and his soldiers.

That was the moment Firaun finally believed and cried out, "None has the right to be worshipped but Allah. And I am one of those who believe."

But it was too late.

"Now you believe, Firaun, when time and again you refused to believe!" replied Allah. "This day, We shall deliver your dead body from the sea that you may be a sign and a warning to those who come after you."

Not long after their exodus from Egypt, the Israelites complained of hunger and thirst, so Musa prayed to Allah for help. Allah then sent down manna, an edible fungus, and quails, flightless birds that were easy to catch, but they soon began to complain again. This time, they demanded variety – herbs, lentils, wheat, cucumbers, garlic, onions, and other good things that grow on the earth. They also wanted to leave the desert and settle down.

Inspired by Allah, Musa led them to the land of Canaan, present-day Lebanon, Syria, Jordan, and Israel. And although they knew Allah had chosen this land for them, they were afraid to enter the main city. How could they be sure Allah would grant them victory over its inhabitants, they queried?

"O Musa!" they said. "There are powerful people in this land. We cannot enter while they are there." And they asked Musa to send two of his most trusted men, Yusha and Kalab, to enter first and fight them while they sat outside the city gates waiting.

Musa despaired of them. "O my Lord!" he prayed. "I have power only over myself and my brother. Separate us from those who are rebellious and disobey Thee."

Allah then declared the Holy Land forbidden for forty years. So, for forty years the Bani Israel wandered in the wilderness, enduring the hardships they had brought upon themselves by repeatedly disbelieving and disobeying Allah's Messenger. Finally, they settled in a land of abundance, but their troubles were far from over. There, they came across people devoted to idol worship.

"O Musa!" they said. "Make for us a god like theirs."

Musa was appalled. After all their suffering; after struggling so desperately to be free; and despite Allah's clear Messages and His favours, their faith was so shallow.

"O my people!" he said. "You know not the Majesty and Greatness of Allah and what He has commanded you – to

103

worship none but Him alone, the One and Only True God of all that exists. These people you wish to follow will surely be punished because they worship idols. All their worship is in vain. Have you forgotten already how Allah saved you from Firaun who was inflicting the worst torments upon you?"

Leading the rebellious Bani Israel was a challenging task for Musa. Their waywardness often caused him great anguish. They even spread rumours about his physique because, unlike them, Musa never undressed himself in public. They thought nothing of bathing naked together in the river, and because Musa never did, they teased him endlessly, insinuating he covered himself to hide a deformity. But then one day, something strange occurred that put an end to their allegations.

Musa came across a secluded part of the river and decided to take a bath. Confident he was completely alone, he removed all his clothes, put them on a large stone and stepped into the water. When he had finished bathing, he reached for his clothes, but the rock suddenly lifted itself and fled, taking his clothes with it.

Musa picked up his staff and ran after it shouting, "O stone! Give me back my clothes!" But the stone moved on until it came across a group of Bani Israel who saw Musa naked for the very first time; and contrary to their suspicions, his body was flawless and perfectly formed. When the stone finally stopped, Musa hurriedly dressed himself. He then began hitting the stone with his staff to punish it.

"You who believe, be not like those who annoyed Musa, but Allah cleared him of that which they alleged, and he was honourable before Allah." Holy Qur'an, 33: 69.

Despite countless miracles, Bani Israel repeatedly disobeyed God and His noble Messenger. When a member of their tribe was murdered, they asked Musa to find out who had committed the terrible crime. In reply, inspired by Allah, Musa told them to sacrifice a cow.

"What has a cow to do with the murder of this man? And what kind of cow?" they asked, possibly with no intention of obeying.

Finally, after receiving a clear description of the cow, they slaughtered it. Inspired by Allah, Musa told them to strike the murdered man with part of the cow; and the man spoke and revealed the identity of his killer.

Now, Allah had appointed forty nights of meditation for Musa. Before leaving, he asked his brother Harun to take command until his return.

At the appointed time and place, Musa knelt and prayed, "O my Lord! Show Yourself that I may look upon You."

"You cannot see Me," Allah answered. "But look upon the mountain. If it remains standing still in its place, then you will see Me."

As Allah drew near, the mountain crumbled into dust. Overcome by the brilliance of the Divine Light, even though he had seen only the slightest glimpse of Allah as small as the tip of his little finger, Musa became unconscious. When he recovered, he said, "Glory be to Thee! I turn to Thee in repentance, and I am the first of the believers."

"O Musa! I have chosen you above men through My Messages and by speaking to you. So hold on to that which I have given you and be of the grateful."

Allah then enlightened him with the criteria of right and wrong, truth and falsehood, and gave him the Tablets of His Commandments, which He had engraved.

"Hold on to these with firmness and tell your people to follow them."

Little did Musa know that during his absence, incited by a man named Samiri, his people had collected all the gold ornaments they had brought with them from Egypt and melted them down to make an idol – the image of a calf that made a low, mooing sound as the wind swept through its hollow body.

Now, it so happened that during the exodus from Egypt, Samiri, chief of the Samiri clan, also joined them. It is believed he originally belonged to a nation of cow-worshippers who somehow reached Egypt and pretended to follow the religion of Bani Israel, but wherever he came from, he was most certainly a hypocrite.

Imagine Musa's horror when he returned from the wilderness, spiritually enlightened by his meeting with his Lord, to find his people worshipping a golden calf. In his anger he threw the Sacred Tablets to the ground and grabbed Harun by the beard.

"Brother, let me go!" Harun pleaded. "And don't blame me. I tried to stop them, but they threatened to kill me."

After severely reprimanding his people, Musa showed them the Tablets of Allah's Commandments. He reminded them of Allah's countless blessings and favours. He also warned them of His wrath. While some repented, others defiantly continued to worship the golden calf. Allah then gave orders to kill the idol worshippers. The repentant, however, were reluctant to obey the order because some of the guilty were close relatives.

"Is it true," they questioned, "that Allah has commanded us to kill our own kith and kin? We will not believe you until we see Allah clearly."

Instantly, they were all struck by lightning. Musa prayed for them and Allah, the Most Merciful, revived them. This experience, however, shook the Israelites and made them fear and obey Allah. As for Samiri, for his sin of leading the Bani Israel astray, he was banished. Any contact with him was forbidden. He was thus condemned to the life of a recluse, running to hide himself whenever he saw anyone approaching.

After years of wandering in Sinai, the Israelites reached a valley on the peninsula. They wanted to settle there, but the valley was dry. Allah told Musa to strike a rock with his staff. Twelve springs then gushed forth from the earth, one for each tribe.

The time had come, however, for Musa to leave them, so he appointed Harun and his family to lead the Israelites, urging them all to live in peace and harmony and worship Allah alone.

Musa believed he was the most knowledgeable man of his time. Allah, however, wished to enlighten him and led him to a place where two seas meet; and there he came across a righteous man named al-Khidr. Before setting off on a journey together, al-Khidr warned Musa to be patient and not to question him about any of his actions. Musa agreed.

They walked along the coast and then boarded a boat belonging to villagers who were kind enough not to charge them for the ride. Suddenly, al-Khidr started to hack the boat with an axe-like tool. Musa was horrified.

"These people took us aboard for free, yet you have damaged their boat. Truly, you have done a dreadful thing," said Musa.

Al-Khidr reminded him that he had agreed not to question him. Musa apologised and promised to remain quiet and patient.

Leaving the boat, they walked along the shore where they came across a youth playing with other boys. Al-Khidr seized the youth and killed him. Once again, Musa was shocked. Forgetting his promise, he asked, "Why have you killed an innocent boy? Surely, you have committed a dreadful crime."

Al-Khidr again reminded Musa of his promise. Musa apologised and agreed that if he questioned him once more they must part ways. So, they continued their journey until they reached a village. They were tired and hungry, but when they asked the villagers for food they refused and closed their doors.

As they were leaving, they came across a wall that was in a bad state, about to collapse. Al-Khidr set to work to repair it. Musa was annoyed and once again complained. The villagers had showed no kindness, so why did he repair the wall for nothing? He could have demanded payment for it so they could buy food.

"It is time for us to part," said al-Khidr, "but before we go our separate ways, let me tell you the reason for my actions. The boat I damaged belonged to poor, believing men who earned their living from it. Their king was a tyrant and had plans to seize every seaworthy boat for himself. I damaged theirs so that he would reject it. They could later repair it and use it again.

"The youth I killed was a wicked disbeliever who had harmed others and would have brought disgrace upon his God-fearing parents. We hoped Allah would give them a noble, affectionate son in his place.

"As for the wall, it belonged to two orphan boys. Their father had been a good man, a believer, and had left a treasure under the wall for when they came of age. If the wall collapsed before then, someone would discover the orphan's inheritance and steal it. So you see, whatever I did was not of my own accord but inspired by Allah."

Musa now understood, and after apologising, thanked al-Khidr for making him wiser.

Author's Comments

Unfortunately, there have always been people like Firaun in our world. Mean dictators, full of ego and the foolish notion that they can conquer and claim the world; a world that in truth belongs to no man and never will.

"Say: To Whom does the earth belong and whoever is in it? They will say: 'To Allah.' Say: Will you not then remember?" Holy Qur'an, 23: 84, 85.

Islam means peace and submission – submission to the will of Allah, but to submit we must control our psyche ego. Ego plays a game of tug-of-war. It is the enemy within. It leads us astray and is often the cause of conflicts in the world. Men fight for wealth and power, not for justice or freedom. And they fight to keep that power, whatever the cost in human lives and misery. But we should always remind ourselves that *La hawla wala quwwata illa billah* – there is no power nor strength except with Allah.

Firaun's ego led him to believe he was a god. It fuelled his rage and incited him to devise the most diabolical punishments. If only he had had the wisdom to apply reason, that no man made himself or has control or power over the earth and universe, he would not have felt proud and all-important.

Did he never see a farmer planting seeds in the fields? Was it he, Firaun, who sent the sunshine and the rain to make them grow? Was he responsible for their design, and for all the genetic material enclosed in each minuscule seed?

When Egypt suffered terrible plagues, Firaun had no power to rid the land of them. He should have realised and acknowledged then his limitations and helplessness, but he didn't. His mighty ego prevailed, and it deceived him.

Repeatedly, Musa's patience was stretched to the limit by the arrogance, foolishness, rebelliousness, and shallow, shifting faith of his people. But like all the noble Messengers he remained steadfast. It is a test of our faith to believe in Allah and follow His commands whatever our circumstances may be. We cannot have faith one day and change our mind the next. Allah forbids it.

From the story of Qarun, we learn that man is mistaken if he thinks his wealth is the fruit of his own labour. Only Allah gives, according to His will, to whomever He wills, whether it is health, strength, wealth, intelligence, or success. A wise man acknowledges Allah's bountiful favours and shows gratitude openly and in private. He gives Zakat regularly and shares his wealth, keeping enough for his own needs and pleasure. And he knows that to have worldly wealth is also a test. Does the rich man use his money wisely? Does he share it? Or does he squander it on himself, believing it to be his and his alone?

Through Musa's encounter with al-Khidr, we learn that things are rarely what they seem. Since we have limited knowledge and lack wisdom and insight, our thinking, our calculations, assumptions, and conclusions are usually wrong. Beware of assumptions! All too often they lead us astray.

We do not know what Allah intends for us. He works in mysterious ways; and nothing He does is without purpose. Musa was extremely angry with the stone for running off with his clothes, but Allah's purpose was to protect his reputation and prevent further ridicule.

Finally, no one lives forever. So, we should try our best to fill each day with worship and honourable deeds and avoid procrastination. Live each day as if it is the last and do what we can do today. Do not leave it till the very last moment, as Firaun did, to believe, do good or ask for forgiveness.

Prophet Dawud

(alayhi as-salaam – peace be upon him)

Long after their massive exodus from Egypt, the Israelites had degenerated into a nation devoid of faith and morality. They committed appalling sins and even killed the prophets Allah sent to guide them. As a result, they were weak, vulnerable, and easily defeated by the Amalekites, descendants of Amalek, the grandson of Yaqub's twin brother, al-Eis (Esau), who had refuted the covenant with Allah and gone his own way.

The Amalekites relentlessly pursued and persecuted the Israelites, enslaving the women, killing the men, and snatching their wealth and property. Only when the Amalekites conquered and ruled over them did the Israelites begin to think seriously about their plight and how to redress it. At the same time, Allah sent a Messenger called Shamm'il (Samuel) to guide them. They asked Shamm'il to send them a king who would lead them in battle, to fight in the way of Allah.

"Is it not likely that if you are called to fight for the sake of Allah you will turn back as you have done before?" was Shamm'il's honest reply.

"What reason have we not to fight?" they asserted. "We have been attacked and driven from our homes and we have lost our sons in battle."

Allah thus appointed Talut (Saul) as their king, but the Israelites refused to accept him.

"How can he be our king?" they argued. "He is an ordinary man like us. He has no riches, no power and no kingdom."

Shamm'il explained that Allah had endowed Talut with strong physique, knowledge, and wisdom; and as a sign of his kingship the Ark of the Covenant would be returned to them. The Ark of the Covenant was a wooden, gold-covered chest, a relic left behind by Musa's people, which the Israelites used to place at the frontline of the battlefield, believing it would grant them victory.

When the Amalekite king fought and overcame them, he seized the Ark, but wherever he took it, it brought him bad luck. Five cities that he entered with the Ark became completely desolate due to epidemics or other catastrophe, so he decided to get rid of it before it brought him more misfortune. He loaded it onto two bullocks and then whipped them, sending them running into the wilderness.

By Allah's command, angels took control of the bullocks and drove them to Talut's doorstep. The Ark of the Covenant was thus returned as Shamm'il had promised and the Israelites accepted Talut as their king. Almost immediately after, King Talut decided to mount an attack on the Amalekites even though the weather was unbearably hot.

"Allah is going to test you by a river," he warned his soldiers. "Whoever drinks from it is not one of my men, but whoever does not drink is surely one of mine."

Overcome with thirst, all but few of the soldiers drank from the river. Talut and his small band of men then crossed the river and marched towards the battlefield. Some were already disheartened, claiming it would be impossible to overcome the Amalekite army. Others rallied with the reminder that by Allah's will, many small groups had overcome vast armies.

Now facing the enemy, they prayed, "Our Lord! Give us patience, set our feet firmly and make us victorious over the disbelieving people."

In those times, it was customary to commence battle with single combat. The chief of one army or a soldier of exceptional strength and valour would challenge the chief or a distinguished soldier of the other army, and they would fight to the death. This served to boost the soldiers' morale. It also determined at the onset of a battle which army was stronger. And so, when Talut's measly army faced the Amalekites, Jalut stepped forward and challenged Talut to send one of his men.

No one came forward. No one dared, for Jalut was no ordinary soldier, but a giant and a ruthless beast of a man.

Dawud bravely facing the mighty Jalut
with only a sling for a weapon.

Talut offered his beautiful daughter in marriage to any soldier who would fight him. Moments of silence! And still no one came forward. Then, to everyone's surprise, a young man shouted, "I will fight him!"

Laughter echoed from the enemy's side, and Talut's men shook their heads in disbelief. The youth must be joking, they thought. But far from it! Dawud, which was the young lad's name, was determined to meet the challenge. King Talut was impressed by his stupendous courage, but feared he was too young and too small.

"Let a strong man come forward," he said. "You are no match for that mighty warrior."

Dawud was still eager to prove he was. "I once killed a lion to save my father's sheep," he asserted. "And on another occasion, I killed a bear. I am not afraid of any man or beast." He then begged the king not to judge him by his appearance.

So, the king agreed to let him fight. "My brave soldier," he said, "if you are willing to fight, then may Allah protect you and grant you victory."

Dressed in battle armour and with sword in hand, Dawud stood, ready to fight, but having never worn armour before, it felt cumbersome and restricted his movements, so he took it off. He returned the sword as well. He did not need it. He had his own simple weapon, a sling, and a leather pouch filled with pebbles. Understandably, Talut was worried. How, he wondered, was Dawud going to defend himself with a sling? And against Jalut of all men!

"Allah who protected me from the jaws of the lion and the claws of the bear will certainly protect me from this barbarian," Dawud assured him, boldly striding off towards the enemy.

When Jalut set eyes on Dawud, he was highly amused. "Have you come out to play war games with one of your playmates?" he roared. "Or are you tired of life already? Come then, and I'll cut off your head with one swipe of my sword."

"You may have armour, shield and sword," Dawud boldly shouted back, "but I face you in the name of Allah Whose laws you have mocked and denied. Today, you will see, it is not the sword that kills, but the will and power of Allah."

Mighty words indeed! And so saying, Dawud took his sling, carefully placed a pebble in it and aimed at Jalut. With the speed of a bullet, the pebble shot from the sling and hit Jalut on the forehead, right between the eyes. So forceful was the blow that he slumped to the ground, blood gushing from his head. Dawud rushed forward, took Jalut's sword from his hand and slew him with it. Seeing their mighty warrior lifeless on the ground, the soldiers fled. Talut and his men followed in hot pursuit, killing every soldier within reach.

Dawud became a hero overnight, the Israelites regained their lost honour and glory, and Talut kept his promise. Dawud married his beautiful daughter, Miquel. The king also appointed him as his Chief Advisor. But fame and good fortune did not turn his young head. Dawud was so modest and firm in faith that after his victory over Jalut he went alone into the desert to meditate and pray, and to thank

Allah for all His favours. Routinely, he prayed and fasted on alternate days.

One day, Dawud sensed a change in the king's attitude towards him. When he discussed it with his wife, she began to cry.

"O Dawud! I can never keep any secret from you," she said. She then told him that her father was jealous of his popularity and feared he might lose his kingdom to him. She advised him to always be on his guard.

Overwhelmed by this news, Dawud went away to meditate and pray that Talut's good nature would prevail over the devilish thoughts and feelings. The following day, Talut summoned Dawud and told him Canaan had gathered its forces and was marching towards their kingdom. He ordered him to force the enemy back and not to return unless victorious. Dawud suspected this might be a ruse to be rid of him. If the enemy did not kill him then one of Talut's henchmen would. Nevertheless, he set out with his troops and fought back the Canaan army.

Dawud's victory, however, only increased Talut's fears. This son-in-law was proving to be too clever and too popular, so he plotted to kill him. The moment Miquel came to know about the pernicious plot, she hurried to warn her husband. Taking food and other necessities with him, Dawud mounted his camel and fled. He hid in a cave, and later his brothers and their followers joined forces with him.

Talut's army was now divided. If his position and power were not threatened before, they certainly were now, so he had no alternative but to fight a battle against Dawud and his followers. He set off with his puny army, but after travelling for hours on end they were exhausted and decided to rest.

While they lay deeply asleep, Dawud crept stealthily up to Talut, quietly drew his sword from its scabbard and cut off a piece of his garment. He then nudged him to awaken him.

"O King!" he said. "You come to fight me, but I have no animosity, nor do I wish to kill you. If I did, I would have killed you just now while you were asleep. I could have cut off your head instead of this piece of your garment. My mission is that of peace and goodwill, not hostility."

Talut at once realised that all his doubts had been unfounded and begged Dawud for forgiveness. With renewed confidence in his son-in-law, the king abandoned his battle plans. Sometime later, however, Talut was killed in battle and Dawud succeeded him. Allah had already chosen Dawud to be a prophet. Now he was also a king.

He was a wise, just, and righteous ruler who brought peace and prosperity to his people. Allah gave him the scriptures, the psalms of worship and praise, and endowed him with a sweet voice and the ability to understand the language of birds. The birds obeyed him and joined in his songs of praise, glorifying Allah at sunset and sunrise, as did the mountains.

"Remember Our servant Dawud, a man of strength who always turned to Us. We made the mountains join him in glorifying Us at sunset and sunrise; and the birds, too, in flocks, all echoed his praise. We strengthened his kingdom; We gave him wisdom and a decisive way of speaking." Holy Qur'an, 38: 17-20.

Allah made iron soft for him so that he could make coats of protective armour for himself and his soldiers, for they had to fight numerous battles against powerful enemies. Dawud divided his working day into four parts – one for his livelihood, personal affairs, and rest; one for prayer and meditation; one for listening to the problems of his subjects; and one for preaching Allah's Divine Message. He dedicated his life to worship and to singing praises to Almighty Allah.

Author's Comments

Dawud clearly acknowledged that greatness belongs only to Allah when he said to Jalut, "It is not the sword that kills, but the Will and Power of Allah."

La hawla wala quwwata illa billah – there is no power nor strength except with Allah.

And he kept a balance between all his activities; an example we can learn from, to ensure that in our daily lives we keep a harmonious balance between worship, work, rest, and play.

When King Talut began to doubt Dawud's intentions, his misgivings were based on suspicion and assumptions fuelled by jealousy. Jealousy is a deadly sin that can lead to violence and self-destruction. And jealousy is another thief. It steals our peace of mind. It can steal our happiness and friends. A manifestation of our resentment of what Allah has bestowed on others, it can also rob us of our faith. Those who trust in Allah accept that He gives to whom He wills, according to His wisdom and His perfect plan.

"Whatever of mercy (i.e. goodness) Allah may grant to humanity, none can withhold it; and whatever He may withhold, none can grant it thereafter. And He is the All-Mighty, the All-Wise." Holy Qur'an, 35: 2.

Unfortunately, we all tend to make assumptions. Even worse, we make judgements and act according to those assumptions, whereas judgements should be based on facts and truth alone. So beware! Assumptions are the devil's guesses, wild, misleading, and often wicked. They can cause family quarrels and end friendships. May Allah give us wisdom to seek only the truth and to act with perspicacity.

Prophet Sulaiman

(alayhi as-salaam – peace be upon him)

Prophet Dawud had a son named Sulaiman (Solomon) who from early childhood was exceptionally intelligent and wise, at times wise beyond his years.

One day, the king was listening to the people's problems and disputes in open court when two men came to him, a farmer, and a shepherd. The farmer demanded compensation because the shepherd's goats had strayed into his field at night and destroyed all the crops. Having established that the value of the goats was equal to the value of the crops, King Dawud ordered the shepherd to give all his goats to the farmer, which according to the law was a just verdict.

As they were leaving the court, the two men met Sulaiman who asked them if the king had resolved their dispute. When they told him about the king's decision, Sulaiman remarked, "If I had judged this case my verdict would have been different and would have benefitted both of you." He then went to his father and told him the same.

"What is this verdict you have in mind that would benefit both men?" Dawud asked.

"Wouldn't it be more just and fair if the herd of goats were given to the farmer so he could benefit from their milk and other produce, and the field given to the shepherd so he could cultivate and grow crops? And when the field is as it was before the goats ruined it, then the property of both men should be returned to them."

King Dawud was so impressed by Sulaiman's wisdom, he recalled the farmer and the shepherd and announced a new verdict according to his son's ingenious proposal.

Another incident when Sulaiman demonstrated extraordinary ingenuity was the dispute between two women. Each had given birth to a baby boy about the same time, but one night, a wolf sneaked into the village and snatched one of the babies. The older of the two mothers, the one whose infant the wolf had devoured, then took the younger woman's baby and claimed it was hers. When questioned, she put on such a clever act, wailing, and pleading, that even the elders of the village were inclined to believe her. The birth mother, of course, insisted the baby was hers, but did not know how to prove it. And so, the dispute continued.

Finally, they brought the case to King Dawud's court. After listening attentively to each woman in turn, the king awarded the baby to the older woman. Sulaiman, however, instinctively felt that this was not a just decision and asked his father's permission to call the women back to court. Immediately, he summoned one of the guards and ordered him to slice the baby in two and give one half to each of them.

Resolving the dispute between the
two women and the baby.

The woman who had falsely claimed the baby was hers cringed with fear and guilt but did not say a word. The sight of the mighty sword, however, was too much for the baby's real mother. Screaming hysterically, she fell to her knees.

"No! Stop! I beg you! Please do not harm the baby," she pleaded. "Let her keep him." And she pointed to the older woman.

Sulaiman's clever ruse worked, for it was now evident who the baby's real birth mother was. Such was Sulaiman's wisdom!

Allah gave Sulaiman the power to command the winds and understand the language of animals and birds. Once, as they were marching towards the country of Askalon, a tiny ant saw the approaching army and sent out a warning cry to all the other ants.

"Run! Run to your homes otherwise, unknowingly, Sulaiman and his army might crush you."

Sulaiman heard the ant's cry and smiled to himself. He was glad the ant knew he was a prophet and would never intentionally harm any of Allah's creatures. He thanked Allah for saving the ants and asked Him to inspire him to be righteous, obedient, and forever thankful.

Sulaiman was an immensely powerful king whose authority and influence extended far beyond his own kingdom. Allah made the jinn obey him. There were jinn that dived into the sea for pearls or worked in his copper mines. Others were craftsmen who built grand rooms in his palace, made huge brass cauldrons and basins as large as reservoirs. He also had a mighty army, divided into different battalions of men, jinn, animals and birds, and a cavalry of magnificent horses.

Sulaiman had a great passion for beautiful horses. One afternoon, especially for his pleasure, the horses were paraded before him. When the display was over, he called them back so that he could enjoy them a little longer. So engrossed was he, stroking and admiring them, that he forgot the afternoon prayers. Only when the sun had set did he realize that his love of horses had made him forget Allah. Deeply ashamed and full of remorse, he promised never to indulge in his passion for horses again. But Allah wanted to try him in faith and obedience, so He took his throne from him for a while.

"O my Lord!" he prayed. "Forgive me and bestow upon me such a dominion as none shall have after me. Verily, You are the giver of all things." And because it was His plan, Allah pardoned him, and later returned him to the throne.

Sulaiman was a strict disciplinarian, especially in military affairs. One morning, after muster call, he was inspecting his army when he discovered one of his birds, the hoopoe, was missing. Severe punishment awaited it unless it had a good reason for being absent. Soon after, the hoopoe returned and explained that it had been scouting the land of Saba (Sheba), now known as Yemen.

Allah had blessed the people of Saba, the descendants of Saba Abd Shams, with all conceivable comforts. In return for these blessings, they had pledged belief in the One True God, and to obey His commandments. For a time, they were obedient, but then gradually became so engrossed in worldly affairs they began to neglect their duty to Allah. They even went as far as to deny Him. Allah sent thirteen prophets in succession to warn them, but despite all their efforts to bring them back to the right path, the people of Saba persisted in their arrogant, careless ways.

They had two gardens, superabundant in all kinds of fruits, and watered by a series of canals fed by a dam. One day, by Divine Decree, the gates of the dam opened, flooding, and completely ruining the magnificent gardens. Retribution for their ingratitude and disbelief!

"Saba is ruled by a beautiful queen named Bilqis," reported the hoopoe. "She is wealthy and powerful and has a splendid throne, but Satan has entered her heart and the hearts of all her people. They worship the sun instead of Almighty Allah."

Sulaiman was deeply troubled by the hoopoe's report and immediately wrote a letter to the queen, respectfully urging her to give up sun-worship and worship the One True God. On receiving the letter, the queen summoned her advisors.

"He begins his letter: In the Name of Allah, the Lord of Mercy, the Bestower of Mercy," she told them. "And he says: 'Do not exalt yourselves above me but come to me as true

believers who submit to Allah.' So, what are your thoughts?"
she asked.

If Sulaiman was planning to conquer them, they should
confront him in battle. "We have a strong army," they
boasted, "but it is for you to decide and to give the command.
So consider carefully."

Now, Bilqis was wise enough to know that peace and
friendship are better than war, which only brings destruction
and humiliation. So, as a goodwill gesture, she decided to
send her envoys to Sulaiman with lavish gifts.

Dazzled by the splendour of Sulaiman's palace, the envoys
bowed respectfully and presented the queen's gifts, but
Sulaiman refused them.

"Allah has given me a prosperous kingdom and made me a
prophet. I do not accept compliments or favours. My sole
purpose is to spread belief in the Oneness of Allah."

He told them to take the gifts back to their queen and to
warn her that if she did not leave sun-worship he would
attack her kingdom and drive her and all her people from
their land. The envoys knew this was no empty threat. They
had noticed his army. It was massive, and matchless. So, in
an uneasy state of mind, they returned to their queen and
conveyed Sulaiman's message.

Bilqis at once decided to meet this remarkable king and
sent word to him that she was coming. Sulaiman wanted
to impress her, to win her favour and persuade her to

worship Allah alone, so as soon as he knew she was on her way, he asked his jinn to fetch her throne. The queen duly arrived, and Sulaiman received her with great pomp and ceremony.

"Is your throne like this?" he asked, pointing to her throne, which he had slightly altered just to confuse her.

Bilqis was speechless. It looked so much like her throne; she was inclined to believe it was. But how could it be? Hers was in her palace hundreds of miles away.

"It appears to be the very same," she discreetly replied.

Sulaiman then led her into a great hall laid with a shimmering glass floor with water flowing beneath it. She lifted her gown above her ankles as she entered, thinking it was a pool of water. Imagine her astonishment when Sulaiman told her she was actually walking on glass! She was so impressed by everything she saw that it did not take her long to realise she was in the company of a most remarkable man. Not only was he knowledgeable and wise and the ruler of a great kingdom, but he was also a prophet for sure. She renounced sun-worship, accepted his religion, and asked her people to do the same.

Sulaiman was undoubtedly a king of unmatched status and power, but when he was just fifty-three years old, he learned that his death was imminent. He was not afraid of death but feared the construction of a mosque started by his illustrious father, King Dawud, would come to a halt after his own demise. The jinn were rebellious by nature and only kept working when they knew he was watching over them, so he devised a way of ensuring the work would continue even after his death.

When the time for his death was near, Sulaiman entered the mihrab, the seat of authority in the palace that had a transparent glass surround, allowing the jinn to see him clearly. As was his routine, he sat leaning on his wooden staff in a position of worship. At the appointed time, his soul was taken, but supported by the staff his body remained in the same position so that it appeared to the jinn he was engrossed in prayer.

In this state of worship, the jinn would not dare to come close and peek at him, so they kept on working until the building was complete. Allah then commanded a little worm to enter the wooden staff; and when it had gnawed through all the wood, Sulaiman's body fell to the ground. Only then did everyone realise he was dead.

Author's Comments

Sulaiman was not only a prophet, but a very prosperous king. However, his wealth and power did not make him proud, although on one occasion his passion for horses almost cost him his throne. Liking something is one thing; having a passion for it is quite a different matter.

All five prayers, Fajr, Zohr, Asr, Maghrib, and Isha, are compulsory, but Allah warns us to be especially mindful of the Fajr and Asr prayers. According to Hadith by Abu Hurairah (may Allah reward him), angels come to us in succession by day and night, and they all get together at the time of the Fajr and Asr prayers. Then those who have stayed with us overnight ascend to Allah, Who asks them, "How have you left My slaves?"

If they reply, "We left them while they were praying and we came to them while they were praying;" and if, while praying, anyone says 'Ameen' after the recitation of surah al-Fatihah at the same time the angels in Heaven say 'Ameen,' then all his or her past sins will be forgiven. Only Allah knows.

Another Hadith, narrated by Sahih Al-Bukhari, warns that whoever deliberately misses the Asr prayer, all his virtuous deeds will be lost. Only Allah knows.

Gambling and intoxication are the devil's clever ploys to lead us astray. Passion or obsession for a pastime or hobby can also distract us from the remembrance and worship of Allah. So, if we have a passion for something, it might be wise to assess whether our passion is taking up most of our time, energy and attention to the exclusion or detriment of priorities like prayers, studies, family and social obligations, and domestic duties.

This story also teaches us to be kind to animals and that even the smallest creatures have intelligence and feelings. And because they are part of Allah's creation, animals have every right to share our world.

Prophet Yunus

(alayhi as-salaam – peace be upon him)

Prophet Yunus was born in Syria. Well-known for his wisdom and righteousness, he received the Divine Call to go to Nineveh, the capital of the Assyrian Empire, to guide its people back to the right path. Nineveh was a prosperous city with beautiful buildings and palaces. Its people, however, indulged in shameless, wicked pursuits and worshipped idols. Yunus tried his utmost to persuade them to mend their ways and believe in the One True God. He warned them of grave consequences if they did not. For forty years, he preached but to no avail. The people only scoffed and jeered at him.

"For years, our fathers and forefathers have worshipped these gods and no harm has ever come to us," they bragged.

When Yunus gave them a final warning that punishment from Allah would surely come, they recklessly replied, "Let it come! Let it come!"

Exasperated, Yunus decided to leave them to their fate and set off towards the coast. As he approached the outskirts of the city, the sky suddenly turned bright red as if on fire. They are now doomed, he said to himself.

Inside the city, the people were in a state of panic. They had listened to stories about the destruction of 'Ad and Thamud, and of Nuh's flood. Had Yunus been right all along, and was theirs to be a similar fate, they wondered? Overcome by fear, they all gathered on a hill and prayed aloud, begging Allah for mercy and forgiveness; and because they were sincerely repentant, He withheld the impending punishment.

"Was there any community that believed (when it saw the punishment) and their faith (at that moment) saved it, except the people of Yunus (Jonah) when they believed? We removed the torment of disgrace in the life of this world and permitted them to enjoy for a while." Holy Qur'an, 10: 98.

Overjoyed, and relieved that Allah had spared them, they looked around for Yunus. Now more than ever, they needed him to guide them and keep them on the right path, but he was nowhere to be found.

Meanwhile, Yunus had boarded a small ship that was sailing out to sea. All day the sea was calm, but when night came they ran into a terrible storm. Ferocious winds and rain pounded the heavily laden ship and mighty waves as high as mountains threatened to capsize it.

Yunus about to be swallowed by a huge fish.

It was a common belief in those times that a perilous predicament like this resulted from someone displeasing Allah. Now at the mercy of the raging sea, the captain made a drastic decision. To safely weather the storm, they would have to throw the guilty person overboard. So, they drew lots to discover who it was. It was Yunus!

They knew Yunas well. He was a righteous man, a man of God. So, to be certain, they drew again, and again, but the result was the same. Yunus was a prophet and had let anger and frustration get the better of him. He had abandoned his mission without Allah's permission. Was this his punishment? Only Allah knows.

Yunas threw himself into the hostile sea and the cruel waves tauntingly and violently tossed him until finally he was drawn under. But he did not drown. A huge fish saw his limp body drifting slowly downwards and swallowed him up into its belly. When he realized where he was and that he was still alive, he prayed repeatedly: *"La illaha illa antu subhanak inni kuntu min adh-dhalimeen.* There is no God but You. Glory be to You. Truly, I was in the wrong." Holy Qur'an, 21: 87.

Allah heard his prayer and commanded the fish to spew him out onto the shore where he lay limp, sick, and exhausted. When at last he opened his eyes, he saw a gourd tree providing him with shade from the burning sun and fruit to eat. He knew it was a blessing from his Lord and was truly thankful.

Gradually, he regained health and strength. When he made his way back to Nineveh sometime later, he was overwhelmed by the warm welcome he received, and amazed to see how the people had changed. Not only had they left their wicked ways, but they also believed in Allah and openly worshipped Him.

Author's Comments

A unique story indeed! The story of a nation Allah saved from the fate He had decreed for it, and of a prophet who disobeyed Him.

Prophets do not act alone. Their actions are guided by Divine Decree, but being human beings, not angels, they were not infallible and sometimes made mistakes. However, when prophets fall, they immediately seek forgiveness and redemption.

The most reassuring fact and blessing this story conveys is that Allah forgives. He forgives His Messengers and their people. He forgives all those who are truly repentant. We are all guilty of sin. Sometimes, we do wrong unintentionally, often unknowingly. And there are times when what we say causes trouble or pain simply because our words are carelessly chosen or misunderstood; and words spoken in jest are not always appreciated.

So, we should not only think before we do anything, but think carefully before we speak. There is a wise saying: *If your feet slip you can usually recover your balance, but if your tongue slips you cannot take back your words.* To err is human, and forgiveness is one of Allah's attributes. We should therefore learn to forgive others as well as ourselves. Forgiveness helps to spread peace and goodwill.

Prophet Ilyas

(alayhi as-salaam – peace be upon him)

Over time, the kingdom of Bani Israel became divided into two states, Yahudiyah (Judah) and Israel. Ahab, the king of Israel, lived in the capital city, Samaria, with his wife Isabelle who was an ardent devotee of their so-called god, Ba'l. Ahab endorsed his wife's idolatrous beliefs and built for her a huge altar dedicated to her god.

King Ahab was neither good nor wise. Not only was he an idol-worshipper, but he was also a tyrant, claiming wealth and power by any means. Evil prevailed and anyone who dared to mention the worship of Allah, the One True God, was persecuted. Allah thus appointed Ilyas as a Messenger to Ahab and his people; to preach to them and urge them to embrace pure monotheism, and to warn them of severe retribution if they did not change their wicked ways. Ilyas tried his utmost to make them understand that Ba'l and all the other false gods they worshipped were powerless to prevent any catastrophe, but they paid no heed.

King Ahab had a neighbour, a pious man who had never harmed anyone in his life, but Ahab had him killed and took possession of his land, which included a beautiful garden of fruit trees. Ilyas condemned him for committing such a terrible crime and ordered him to return the land to the slain man's dependants, otherwise Allah would punish him. "And you will be killed in this garden, if you do not return it," he added.

Furious with Ilyas for daring to admonish him, Ahab threatened to kill him. His wife was also plotting to have him killed because of his derogatory remarks against Ba'l. When Ilyas came to know about their evil plans, he took refuge in a cave on the outskirts of Samaria. There he stayed for a considerable length of time, imploring Allah to afflict the people of Ahab with a disaster that would make them abandon idol-worship and turn towards Him, the True God.

When a dreadful drought spread throughout the entire kingdom, Ilyas decided it was time to return to Ahab and his people, to call them again to the right path. He told them the famine was the result of their disobedience to Almighty Allah, but as ever they were foolishly defiant. They claimed theirs was the true religion and boasted that Ba'l had over one hundred apostles to prove it. Ilyas then asked them to gather the apostles to offer sacrifices in the name of Ba'l, and he would offer a sacrifice in the name of Allah. The offering completely consumed by a fire from heaven would indicate the true religion.

Everyone gathered on a mount, and from morning till late afternoon the false apostles of Ba'l offered their sacrifices, but not a single sacrifice was touched by fire. Ilyas then offered his sacrifice, and instantly a fire came from heaven and burnt it to ashes. Before everyone, the truth was manifest. Allah then sent down rain and the long, dreadful drought ended.

While some people believed and fell in prostration, Isabelle, and other ardent followers of Ba'l adamantly refused to abandon their god. They became even more aggressive towards Ilyas, and once again his life was in danger, so he was forced to leave Samaria and go into hiding. Sometime later, he returned and resumed his mission to reform Ahab and his people, but as before, he was met with hostile opposition.

Ahab's rule finally ended when intruders from a foreign land conquered his kingdom. Historians claim that both Ahab and his wife were slain in the beautiful garden he had stolen from his pious neighbour years ago. Only Allah knows.

Author's Comments

What a fatal combination! A king who was despotic, idolatrous, and materialistic.

Materialism is a ploy of the devil. Uncurbed, materialism develops into a cancer-like disease. Cancer destroys the good cells in our bodies; materialism eats away at the goodness in society. People venerate materialism as if it is a god that will satisfy all their needs and bring about everlasting happiness. But it is a great deceiver, an avaricious beast with an insatiable appetite. The moment it has acquired or devoured something; it craves more. And that is why a materialist is never content. His focus on material things leads to insatiable cravings, but like a sumptuous meal, his happiness is fleeting. The taste of delicious food lasts for just moments, and fades when it leaves the tongue. The memory of the taste might linger, but the sensation has gone forever. Cravings have no satisfaction, no end.

However, we live in a material world, not a spiritual one, so material things are an integral and essential part of our existence. But since our aim is to earn a place in Paradise, we need to keep a healthy balance between material and spiritual matters. It might help if we remind ourselves that we leave this world empty-handed. We leave all our possessions and even our body behind. Only our faith and the account of all our deeds will go with us.

Prophet Isa

(alayhi as-salaam – peace be upon him)

Maryam, also known as the Blessed Virgin, was born in the city of Nazareth, Land of Galilee. Her parents, Imran ibn Mathan and Hannah bint Faqudh, belonged to a highly respected clan. A truly devout man, Imran was a priest of Bayt-al-Maqadis, the holy temple in Jerusalem. For years, the couple remained childless, but Hannah continued to hope and pray that she would one day become a mother.

"O Allah! Give me a child who will be the coolness of my eyes and the contentment of my heart," she implored.

When Hannah discovered she was with child, she was overjoyed. Before the baby's birth, however, Imran passed away. Confident her baby was a boy, Hannah promised to dedicate him to the temple, to the worship and service of God. When she gave birth to a baby girl she was confused. How could she now fulfil her promise? How could a girl be of service to God?

Hannah named her baby Maryam and looked after her until she was old enough to be left in the care of her sister whose husband, Zakariyya, was one of the custodians of the temple, thereby fulfilling her promise to God. After much deliberation, Zakariyya was elected the little girl's official guardian. From then on, Maryam would spend her days in the temple, praying and reading the Holy Book, the Taurat, returning to her aunt's house in the evening.

Whenever Zakariyya entered Maryam's prayer room, he noticed she always had food, even fruits out of season. "O Maryam! Where does this food come from?" he asked her one day.

"Allah sends it," she replied. "Allah gives generously without limit to whomever He wishes."

Years later, when Maryam was of marriageable age and suitors were being considered, the angel Jibril (Gabriel) came to her with a Divine Message.

"O Maryam! Allah sends you good news of a Messiah named Isa, son of Maryam. He will be honoured in this world and in the Hereafter and will be close to Allah. He will speak to the people while in the cradle and when he becomes a man. And he will be one of the righteous."

Maryam could not believe what she had just heard. "O my Lord!" she prayed. "How shall I have a child when I am not yet married?"

"It will be so," Jibril assured her. "For Allah creates what He wills. He only commands, 'Be!' And it is. Allah will teach Isa the Books, the Taurat and Injeel (Gospel). And He will make him a Messenger to the Children of Israel."

Jibril then breathed on Maryam, and she conceived a child. When the time came for baby Isa to be born, Maryam went alone into the valley of Bait-ul-Laham. Thirsty, famished, and suffering the agony of labour, she sat down beneath the shade of a palm tree and rested her aching body against its trunk. Allah caused a stream of fresh water to run by her feet, and a voice called out telling her to shake the tree and not to talk to anyone that day. She shook the tree and fresh, ripe dates fell into her lap. The delicious fruit brought relief from the agonising pain, and soon after, baby Isa was born.

Maryam was aware of the penalty for a woman who gave birth to a baby out of wedlock. Death by stoning! But Maryam was no ordinary woman. Allah had chosen her to be the mother of a Messenger. Besides immaculate virtues, she was blessed with enormous courage and conviction. Carrying her new-born baby in her arms, she went back to her people, not to a welcome homecoming, but to hostility. While some scorned, glaring accusingly, others dared to question her, but as commanded, Maryam did not speak. Instead, she pointed to the baby.

"How can we talk to a baby?" they said.

By Allah's will, and to everyone's astonishment, baby Isa spoke. "Truly I am Allah's servant. He has given me the Scriptures and made me a prophet. He has blessed me and

Maryam returning with baby Isa; Isa
blessing the food for the multitude.

ordered me to offer prayers and pay Zakat as long as I live, and to be dutiful to my mother. Peace be upon me the day I was born, the day I die and the day I shall be brought back to life. Allah is my Lord and your Lord, so worship Him Alone. That is the right path."

"The likeness of Isa ... is truly as the likeness of Adam (meaning both were born without a father). He created him from dust and then said, 'Be!' And he was." Holy Qur'an, 3: 58.

Isa grew into a fine young man. He was gentle, kind, and virtuous, but not so the people around him. The Israelites had completely forsaken their religion and with it all sense of morality. Wickedness prevailed. Deceit, jealousy, lying, intrigue, licentiousness! Even learned scholars and religious leaders were corrupt, constantly making changes to Allah's laws and commands in the Taurat to suit their own desire and purpose.

Commanded by Allah, Isa began to preach. "O People! I am a servant and Messenger of Allah. I am a human being like all the prophets sent before me, but Allah has revealed His Book to me and sent me to guide you. Believe in the One and Only God, Allah, and worship none but Him. This is the only way to success in this world and in the Hereafter."

Wicked people do not like to hear the truth, nor are they disposed to change their ways, so Isa's words were not well received. Undaunted, he continued to preach. And to convince the people that he was indeed a prophet, Allah gave him the power to perform miracles. He could heal the lepers, the crippled and the blind. He even brought the dead back to life. On one occasion, he made a bird from clay and then breathed on it, and by Allah's will it became a real bird and flew away. And when his disciples were in a boat on the Sea of Galilee, he walked calmly on the stormy waters to join them and assure them they would be safe.

Isa and his disciples set off one day towards a quiet, deserted place to contemplate and pray. By chance, one of them looked back and was astonished to see a multitude of people following them. The curious, the sick and weary of heart, all eager to be near this compassionate man of miracles; to learn about the One True God and listen to his words of goodness, kindness, and love.

As the sun began to set, the disciples voiced their concern for the people, now weary from the long trek. "Master!" they said. "Shouldn't we send them away so they can find food and drink and a place to sleep?"

"First give them food," Isa replied.

"But we don't have any food," said the disciples. "There is a little boy who has five barley loaves and two fishes with him, but that is all. There are thousands of people here. Should we go into the town and buy food for them?"

"No," Isa calmly replied. "Just sit everyone down in groups of about fifty."

The apostles obeyed, wondering what miracle Isa was about to perform. He took the five loaves and two fishes from the little boy, looked up towards heaven, and asked for Allah's blessing. He then began to break the food into pieces, giving it to his disciples to distribute among the multitude. He continued breaking the food until everyone's hunger was satisfied.

The following is one of Isa's stories, which has a wonderful message – not to judge people according to our means, but theirs; and to see things from their perspective.

The Widow and the Two Mites

One day, Isa happened to be sitting near the collection bowl in the synagogue. He quietly watched as people put money into the bowl when they left – money for the poor and needy. An old woman, a widow, quietly slipped two mites into the bowl, a mite being a coin of the lowest denomination in those days. But when the ostentatiously dressed rich men dropped their coins into the bowl, they ensured they made a loud clanging sound for all to hear.

When everyone had left the synagogue, Isa turned to his disciples and said, "Truly, I tell you, the old woman has put more into the collection bowl than anyone else."

His disciples were baffled. They, too, had seen her slip only two mites into the bowl.

"The others gave of their abundance, but she gave of the little she had. And she gave it to please Allah, not to show off," Isa explained.

Here is another story told by Isa about having compassion for others, even strangers and outcasts, regardless of their colour, race, or creed.

The Good Samaritan

A Jewish man was travelling alone from Jerusalem to Jericho along a desolate and dangerous road where bandits were known to attack, rob, and even kill unsuspecting wayfarers. And sure enough, the ill-fated man was attacked. The bandits beat him up, took all his money, stripped him of his clothes and left him lying on the roadside, half naked, half dead.

Sometime later, a priest came along that way, but when he saw the wounded man, he crossed over to the other side of the road. Bandits must have attacked the unfortunate man, he thought, and might still be lurking nearby. It would be foolish to stop for even a moment on this dangerous stretch of road, so he hurriedly walked on.

Later, a temple servant came along the same road. Like the priest, he had come from the synagogue, from the worship of God, the God of Kindness, Compassion, and Mercy. He saw the wounded wayfarer, even recognised him as a fellow Jew, but did not stop to help him.

Then a Samaritan riding a donkey came along that way. Samaritans were immigrants, despised by the Jews because they were of a different race and religion. But when the Samaritan saw the wounded man, he immediately felt pity for him. There but for the grace of God go I, he thought to himself, meaning, but for the grace of God this could have been me.

Kneeling down, he gently bandaged the wayfarer's wounds as best he could. He then helped him onto his donkey and took him to the nearest inn where he spent the night taking care of him. The next day, he had to continue his journey. After paying the innkeeper for his stay, he gave him extra money and requested him to take care of the wounded man until he regained his health and strength.

"If this money is not enough, I shall pay whatever I owe you next time I come," the Samaritan assured him.

The innkeeper asked him why he was taking so much care of a stranger.

"Do as you would be done by," the Samaritan replied. "In other words, treat others as you would like them to treat you. And for the love of God, do good." He then went on his way.

Here is another amazing story; a parable that alludes to Allah's love for His creation, and His happiness when one who was lost finds his way back to Him.

The Prodigal Son

A rich man had two sons. One day, the younger son asked his father for his share of inheritance so he could go out into the world and seek his fortune. Although he was reluctant to let him go, the father gave him his due share. The son then gathered all his belongings and set off on his long journey to another land. There, he fell into sinful ways and wasted his money on riotous living. When he had spent the last of his inheritance there was a terrible famine in the land. Desperate and destitute, he went to work for a landowner who made him feed the pigs. Often, he was so hungry, he was tempted to eat their food.

My father's servants have bread to eat and even bread to spare while I am starving, he thought. I shall go back to my father and ask his forgiveness. And I shall ask him to keep me as one of his hired servants. So, he journeyed back to his homeland.

"Father, I have sinned and am no longer worthy to be called your son. I beg you to take me as one of your hired servants," he said.

Warmly embracing his long-lost son, he called out to one of his servants and told him to bring the best robe for him. He put rings on his fingers and shoes on his feet. He then ordered the slaughter of the fatted calf.

"Prepare a meal that we may eat and rejoice, for my son who was lost has been found."

When the elder son returned from the fields, he was surprised to hear music and rejoicing coming from the house and asked one of the servants what it was all about.

"Your father is celebrating your brother's return," he told him.

This startling news angered him, and he refused to enter the house. His father came outside and tried to persuade him to join the party, but still he declined.

"All these years I have served you. Never have I disobeyed you, but not once have you offered me so much as a young goat that I may entertain my friends," he protested. "But when my wayward brother returns you kill the fatted calf for him."

"O, my son! You are always with me and all that I have is yours," his father explained. "Your brother is like a sheep that was lost and is found, so wasn't it right to celebrate his return?"

To continue the story of Isa:

Isa travelled from town to town, preaching Allah's Message, helping the poor, and healing the sick. Not surprisingly, he was becoming increasingly popular. So much so, the Jewish leaders began to feel threatened and in danger of losing their control. Soon, everyone would be obeying Isa, not them. Desperate to hold on to power, they devised a wicked plan. At that time, the Romans ruled the land, so they went to the Roman Governor of Damascus whose name was Pilate (Pilot) and complained.

"Isa is a nuisance and a threat to the government," they said. "He doesn't obey the law. He incites people to follow him so that he can raise an army to defeat the Roman Empire and make himself king. You must act immediately if you want to stop this madman from taking over."

Swayed by their clever lies, Pilate ordered his soldiers to find Isa and arrest him. Forewarned of their evil plot, Isa called his disciples and asked them, "Who will be my helpers in Allah's cause?"

"We will be your helpers," his disciples replied. "We believe in Allah and bear witness that we are Muslims, those who submit to Allah and follow Him. And we believe in His Messenger, Isa."

Having said this, they wanted a sign to strengthen their faith. "O Isa! Son of Maryam! Can your Lord send us a table spread with food from Heaven?" they asked. So, Allah sent it down, as a sign and for them to enjoy. It was their last meal together.

Later, Isa was arrested, tried, and sentenced to death by crucifixion. He was kept in a closely guarded cell, but when it was time for the execution the Jewish guards unlocked the cell to find it empty. Isa, it seemed, had disappeared. In fact, Allah had raised him up to Heaven.

Baffled, the soldiers searched high and low until they found a man whom they thought was Isa because he resembled him. They arrested him and crucified him on the cross.

"And because of their saying (in boast), 'We killed the Messiah (Isa), son of Maryam, the Messenger of Allah,' but they killed him not nor crucified him on the cross, but it appeared so to them; and those who differ therein are full of doubts. They have no certain knowledge; they follow nothing but conjecture, for surely, they killed him not. But Allah raised him up (body and soul) unto Himself. And Allah is Ever All-Powerful, All-Wise." Holy Qur'an, 4: 157, 158.

From these verses, it is clear that Isa did not die, but Allah took him, body, and soul, to Heaven. One day, he will return. Supported by angels, he will descend from heaven to complete his life on earth. He will lead the people and bring peace and prosperity; and he will judge people according to the laws of the Qur'an.

Author's Comments

The unique, immaculate conception of Prophet Isa is confirmation that Allah is All Powerful. He made the laws of nature. If He wills, He can change them. He simply commands, and it is.

La hawla wala quwwata illa billah – there is no power nor strength except with Allah.

"It is He Who gives life and causes death. And when He decides a thing, He says to it only 'Be!' And it is." Holy Qur'an, 40: 68.

He is the Creator of the entire universe and all that is in it. His power is limitless. Yet repeatedly, we doubt Allah's power, and whenever we are faced with difficulties, we weigh ourselves down with worry, searching for solutions, when all we need to do is turn to Him.

The miracle of Isa's birth is also a lesson for all humanity; that we should not feel proud if we have sons, daughters, or both. Although we are physically, biologically involved, procreation is the result of God's power and His will.

"...He creates what He wills. He bestows daughters to whomever He wills and sons to whomever He wills; or He bestows both sons and daughters to whomever He wills; and He renders barren whomever He wills. Verily...He is able to do all things." Holy Qur'an, 42: 49, 50.

About Prophet Isa, the Qur'an also says: "And (remember) when Allah will say (on the Day of Resurrection), 'O Isa, son of Maryam! Did you say to men: Worship me and my mother as two gods besides Allah?' He will say: 'Glorified are You! It was not for me to say what I had no right to say. Had I said such a thing You would surely have known it. You know what is in my inner self though I do not know what is in Yours; truly You, only You, are the All-Knower of the hidden and unseen.' This is Isa, son of Maryam (Mary), and this is the truth about him ... It is not befitting that Allah should take a son. Glory be to Him..." Holy Qur'an, 19: 35, 36.

Prophet Muhammad

(Sallallahu alayhi wa-sallam! Peace and
blessings of Allah be upon him!)

Muhammad's lineage goes back sixty generations to Ibrahim's
son, Isma'il. Being the most recent and the last of all the
prophets, far more is known about his life and teachings
than about any other prophet; and because his life was a
model of excellence, every detail has been recorded. Unlike
prophets before him, whose Message was for one nation only,
Muhammad's was the Final Message, sent by God to all
mankind throughout the world.

From early childhood, Muhammad attracted special
attention. All who met him were instantly impressed by his
sweet disposition; and those who knew him acknowledged
and admired his noble character. At an early age, he earned
the titles *al-Amin*, The Trustworthy, and *as-Sadiq*, The
Honest. Although born into a prestigious Arab family, he
was always modest and unassuming. Even in the final years
of his prophethood, when the whole of Arabia was under

his command, he lived a remarkably simple life and had no personal possessions.

No task was beneath his dignity. He would sweep the floors, attend to the animals, and mend his own clothes. He would sit down to eat with the slaves; and when he was travelling, he often allowed his companion, whether servant or friend, to ride his camel while he walked alongside. As for food, he preferred simple barley bread, dates, watermelon, yogurt, cucumber, honey, and milk, and occasionally meat. If he was not hungry, he did not eat.

It was the magnetism of Muhammad's personality, his gentle charm, modesty, sincerity, integrity, dignity, good humour, and tender-heartedness that spread Islam far and wide, and not the sword as some historians claim. Whereas others may have wielded the sword to take control, and stifle freedom of belief, Muhammad and his followers fought only to promote and protect Islam. In no way did they interfere with the dogmas of other faiths, nor did they persecute non-Muslims for their lack of belief in Islam. The following verses are testimony to the Islamic principles of tolerance and goodwill.

"There is no compulsion in religion." Holy Qur'an, 2: 256.

"And do not insult those whom the disbelievers worship besides Allah, lest they insult Allah wrongfully, without knowledge." Holy Qur'an, 6: 108.

The laws of Islam granted liberty of belief and freedom of worship to all who lived in its dominion, so long as they remained allies and refrained from acts of aggression.

Muhammad once made the following appeal to an opposing clan: "Cease all hostility to us and be our allies and we shall be faithful to you; or pay tribute, and we shall secure and protect you in all your rights; or adopt our religion, and you shall enjoy the same privileges as we do."

Muhammad's life was an exemplar for all humanity. He excelled as Commander in Chief, social reformer, moralist, economist, husband, and head of the family. And he was a perfect Muslim. Here is how it all began.

Abdul Muttalib was the chief of the Arab clan of Banu Hashim of the tribe of Quraysh, one of the noblest and most respected tribes of Arabia, distinguished for valour, eloquence, and hospitality. For generations, they had held the honoured position of Guardian of the Haram of Kaaba in Makkah. Abdul Muttalib had six daughters and twelve sons, one of the youngest of them being Abdullah, a handsome, noble youth whom everyone adored. When Abdullah was twenty-five years old, his father arranged his marriage to a woman of excellent virtue. Her name was Aminah, daughter of Wahab bin Abu Manaf, chief of Bani Zahra clan.

Not long after the marriage, Abdullah went to Syria with a trade caravan. On the return journey, feeling a little unwell, he stopped at a relative's house in Medina, known then as Yathrib. Expecting him to quickly recover, his companions stayed with him, but when his health took a sudden and drastic turn for the worse, they hastily returned to Makkah to break the news to his father. Deeply distressed, Abdul

Muttalib immediately sent his eldest son, Harith, to stay with Abdullah until he was well enough to travel back home. Sadly, when Harith arrived it was only to learn his brother had already passed away.

It was a terrible shock. Abdullah was so young and had set off with the caravan hale and hearty and full of enthusiasm. Now everyone was mourning his death. For Aminah, the grief was twofold, for not only had she lost her husband but the father of her unborn child.

It was the Year of the Elephant, so called because in that year Abrahah Al-Ashram, the Christian Governor of Yemen, invaded Makkah with the intention of destroying the Holy Kaaba. Besides being a place of pilgrimage, Makkah was also a vibrant trade centre. Abrahah suggested to the king of the Ethiopian kingdom, of which Yemen was a part, that they build their own sacred house in San'a, the capital of Yemen, in the hope of diverting pilgrims and trade caravans from Makkah to Syria. The king approved the idea, so Abrahah lost no time and immediately ordered the construction of a huge cathedral.

Named al-Qullais or Yemeni al-Kaaba, the cathedral was an architectural wonder, richly adorned with stained glass windows, gold, silver, and precious stones. The elated Abrahah ordered all the Yemeni Arabs to make pilgrimage to al-Qullais instead of to the Kaaba, but the order was ignored. Worse still, it is reported that a man from the Quraysh tribe of Makkah was so infuriated to see the cathedral, he soiled its floor and walls with excrement. Other narrations claim a nomadic tribe set up camp near the cathedral and lit a fire to warm themselves, but the wind was blowing so violently the flames reached the cathedral and it caught fire, causing considerable damage. Either way, whatever the truth of the matter, Abrahah was so enraged, he vowed to take revenge. Stone by stone, he would demolish the Kaaba and extirpate Makkah's illustriousness forever. And with this intent, he raised a massive army and marched towards Makkah.

Abrahah's army, which included about twenty elephants, fought and defeated every opposing tribe along the way. Unhindered, it continued towards Makkah until it came to the settlement of the Banu Khatham tribe. Their leader, Nufail Ibn Habib, fearlessly but foolishly, led his entire tribe against Abrahah's army. Outnumbered and outwitted, they were easily defeated and Nufail was taken prisoner. Initially, Abrahah intended to kill him, but then changed his mind. He was now leading his army into unknown territory where Nufail might prove useful as a guide, so he pardoned him on condition he led the way there onwards.

When the army approached Ta'if, the people of Thaqif went out to meet Abrahah to make peace with him. News had already reached them about the fate of those who had shown resistance, so they were rightly afraid. They also feared Abrahah would destroy the temple of their sacred idol, al-Lat. Their peaceful strategy worked and Abrahah complied.

Pushing forward, Abrahah reached a place called al-Maghmas on the outskirts of Makkah where the Quraysh left their camels and other animals to graze. Abrahah set up camp and ordered his troops to round up the animals. They also drove away about two hundred camels belonging to Abdul Muttalib. Abrahah, now close to his target, sent an emissary to Abdul Muttalib to inform him that he had come only to destroy the Sacred House and not to fight him and his people, unless they challenged him. After listening to his message, Abdul Muttalib asked the emissary to take him to meet Abrahah in person.

Abrahah, although surprised by his uninvited guest, was so impressed by Abdul Muttalib's persona that he stood up to greet him.

"Don't worry," he assured Abdul Muttalib, inviting him to sit beside him. "I have not come to kill you and your people, but only to destroy your Sacred House."

"I have not come to plead with you, but to demand the return of my camels," Abdul Muttalib calmly replied.

Abrahah raised his eyebrows and glared sagaciously at Abdul Muttalib. "When you entered, I was immediately impressed by your fine looks and noble demeanour. In fact, I formed an exceedingly high opinion of you. However, I have now lost all respect for you. You show concern only for your camels even when you know I have come to pull down the Holy Sanctuary of your ancestors, but not a word of protest did you utter, nor did you beg me to spare it."

With his usual dignity and calm, Abdul Muttalib replied, "Since they belong to me, the camels are my concern, but I am not the owner of the Holy Sanctuary, and Allah knows best how to protect His House."

Mahmud refusing to approach the Kaaba.

"Your God cannot protect it from *me*," bragged Abrahah.

Abdul Muttalib returned to Makkah and ordered everyone to flee to the safety of the nearby hills. He then went to the Kaaba and earnestly prayed for victory. "My Lord, we have no strength to fight Abrahah's army, so protect Your House," he pleaded.

The following morning, the people of Makkah watched in awe as the mighty army marched towards the city. They had never seen an elephant before, and one elephant, far bigger than the rest, caught everyone's eye. Its name was Mahmud. Abrahah intended to use Mahmud to demolish the walls of the Kaaba, but as they drew nearer something miraculous happened. Mahmud stopped abruptly and knelt.

After much coaxing, they managed to get him on his feet again, but he would only walk in the direction of Yemen or Syria or towards the east. Whenever they turned him towards the Kaaba he knelt again. Even when they poked and prodded him with long iron spears, Mahmud still refused to move one step towards the Sacred House. And then strangely, suddenly, the sky darkened. Sensing a violent storm was imminent, the elephants began to panic, snorting and trumpeting, their huge bodies swaying uneasily.

Suddenly, ominous black clouds shrouded the sky, or so it seemed. In fact, they were flocks of birds, each carrying a tiny pellet of baked clay in its beak and claws. Without warning, they launched an aerial attack, bombarding the soldiers with the pellets that struck hard, burning deep into their flesh. Some soldiers died on the spot. Others died a slow, agonising death. Only one soldier survived. Blind in both eyes, he remained a street beggar in Makkah for the rest of his long, wretched life. As for Abrahah, he suffered excruciating pain as his infected wounds caused his flesh to decay. Finally, just as he was about to reach home, he breathed his last.

Allah had answered Abdul Muttalib's earnest prayer. He had not only protected His Sacred House, but the city of Makkah and the unborn Prophet of Islam.

In the Year of the Elephant, around midday on a Monday in the month of Rabi-ul-Awwal, 570 C.E. Aminah's baby was born. Since there was no Islamic calendar at the time, there is no exact record of the date. She named her baby son, Muhammad, according to a vision she had seen beforehand.

Abdul Muttalib proudly cradled his new-born grandson in his arms and took him to the Kaaba where he officially named him Muhammad, which means, *Most Worthy of the Highest Praise.*

In those days, it was customary for noble Arab families in Makkah to pay women from the outlying settlements to take care of their infants. Bringing them up in the city was risky. It was overcrowded and diseases spread easily. In the clean, fresh air of the open desert plains the infants had a better chance of growing strong and healthy. They would also learn to speak pure Arabic. Village women thus frequently visited the cities in search of babies, which they would take on contract for an agreed period, usually for good wages.

Soon after Muhammad's birth, village women arrived in Makkah in search of infants to take on contract. One of them was Halima of the tribe of Bani Sa'd bin Bakr accompanied by her husband, Harith bin Abdul-Uzza. Halima was poorer than the other women. Their donkey was feeble and always trailed behind the caravan. Their only milch animal gave no milk, and Halima was so weak she had barely sufficient milk for her own baby, so she feared she stood little chance of securing a contract.

When all the other women had contracted infants and were preparing to leave, Halima was still searching. She had heard about a noble lady called Aminah, that she had a baby boy whom the other women had rejected because he was an orphan. An orphan was not a good prospect as far as wages were concerned. Abdullah left only a few camels and goats and a slave girl named Umm Ayman. But rather than leave empty-handed, and persuaded by her husband, Halima decided to take Aminah's baby whatever the wages.

When she returned to her tent, Halima sat down to suckle the new infant. To her surprise, the milk in her breasts flowed so abundantly she was able to feed him as well as her own baby; and when Harith milked the milch animal, it also had milk in abundance.

"By Allah, you have taken a very special child," he said. And to add to their joy, their donkey trotted so fast it outpaced all the others on the homeward journey.

Two years passed, and little Muhammad, now a healthy, sturdy toddler, was fully weaned. According to the contract, it was time to return him to his mother. Halima had grown so fond of him she was reluctant to part with him and was absolutely delighted when Aminah asked her to keep him a little longer.

When Muhammad was six years old, Aminah took him to Medina to meet her relatives. After a prolonged stay, they set off on the long journey home, but at a place called Abwa on the road between Medina and Makkah, Aminah suddenly became ill. Three days later, she died. After the funeral, Umm Ayman brought the bewildered orphan back to Makkah where his grandfather, Abdul Muttalib, took care of him.

Abdul Muttalib adored him and treated him with great love and kindness. He could not bear to be without him, not even for a moment. Wherever he went, the boy was always by his side. But he was an old man with failing health, and when Muhammad was only eight years old, he too passed away.

How strange was this little boy's fate! One tragedy seemed to follow another. But he was no ordinary child. He was destined to attain such greatness as no man before him. Calmly, bravely, he accepted his circumstances and hid his grief. His new guardian was Abu Talib, his paternal uncle, who also took great care of him. They became inseparable, going everywhere together, even sharing the same bed.

Muhammad grew into a handsome young man. He had a winsome personality, was well-known and well-liked. He was also highly respected for his outstanding character. One of his relatives, a lady called Khadijah, also lived in Makkah, and by virtue of her pure, noble qualities had earned the title, Tahira, *The Pure*. Beautiful, graceful, and the wealthiest of all the Arab women, Khadija was twice widowed, and although she received many proposals of marriage from noble Quraysh families, she declined them all.

A successful businesswoman, Khadijah often owned half the caravan. She was looking for someone to take her merchandise to Syria. At the time, Muhammad was a camel-herder for Khadijah's elder sister, who praised him so much Khadijah decided to offer him charge of her business venture. After consulting with Abu Talib, Muhammad accepted. Khadija was delighted and generously offered him a half share of the profit. Muhammad, along with Khadija's slave, Maisarah, whom she sent to assist him, thus set off on the long journey to the commercial town of Bosra, just short of Damascus.

Maisarah observed Muhammad closely and was immensely impressed by his kindness, good habits, and agreeable manners, his business integrity, and the way he treated him more like a brother than a slave. By the time their caravan returned, Maisarah had become his devoted admirer and lost no time in telling Khadijah all about him. Khadijah was pleased. Muhammad had done very well and made far more profit than she usually earned, so when she listened to Maisarah's report she began to consider a new proposal. Marriage!

Muhammad accepted. Khadijah invited all her clan to the wedding. Muhammad arrived with his uncles, Hamza, and

Abu Talib. His faithful friend, Abu Bakr, and other Quraysh chiefs also attended the ceremony. Muhammad was just twenty-five years old. Khadija was several years older. Their marriage was a blissful one. They had two sons and four daughters. Sadly, both sons died in childhood. Their names were Qasim and Abdullah. The daughters were Zainab, Ruqqiya, Umm-i-Kalthum and Fatima.

When Muhammad was about thirty-five years old, the people of Makkah decided to fortify the Kaaba. As it was in a low-lying area, rainwater from the city collected around it, causing damage to its foundations. Everyone wanted the privilege of rebuilding the House of God, so the chieftains divided the different tasks between the various clans. However, when it came to the placing of the sacred stone, Hajar-i-Aswad, an intense argument broke out over who should perform the task, each tribe coveting the privilege, with the result that tempers flared and swords were drawn, a dispute that raged for four days.

On the fifth day, the most senior member of the Quraysh suggested a way of settling the argument. They would ask the first person to enter the Kaaba through the entrance of Bab-i-Shaeba the next morning to decide the matter. Everyone agreed, so they sat there, waiting, and watching, eager to see the first man to arrive. It was Muhammad. Knowing him to be the epitome of truthfulness, they were happy to let him decide. Muhammad spread his cloak on the ground, placed the stone on it, and asked each tribe to nominate a person to hold a part of the cloak. Together, they lifted the stone and carried it to a niche in the wall of the Kaaba where

Muhammad then set it in its place. Peacefully, amicably, the task was accomplished.

At that time, the Arabian Peninsula was steeped in ignorance and idolatry; and Western Europe was groping its way through the so-called Dark Ages. The entire world was in dire need of a saviour. That saviour had finally arrived.

Deeply perturbed by the moral and religious degradation of his people, Muhammad became more absorbed in prayer and meditation. He would spend the whole month of Ramadan meditating in a cave known as Hira, on the outskirts of Makkah. It was during the month of Ramadan, when Muhammad was about forty years old, that the most exalted of all the angels, Jibril, made his first appearance in the cave.

"Read!" Jibril commanded.

"I cannot read!" Muhammad truthfully replied, whereupon Jibril hugged him so tightly he could barely breathe.

Jibril released him, but once more commanded, "Read!"

Again, Muhammad replied, "I cannot read!" And again, Jibril hugged him tightly.

When he finally released him, he said, "Read! In the name of the Lord Who creates; creates man from a clot. Read! And thy Lord is the Most Bounteous, Who teaches by the pen and teaches man that which he knew not." (Holy Qur'an, 96: 1-5) So saying, Jibril then left.

Muhammad fled the cave, desperate to tell Khadijah what had happened. So shaken was he by the divine revelation that he was still trembling when he reached home. Khadijah comforted him as best she could and assured him that by the grace of Allah no harm would come to him. The next day, she took him to her cousin, Warqa bin Naufal, who had renounced idolatry and become a Christian scholar. He listened attentively as Muhammad related what had happened.

"The angel you saw is the angel Jibril who brings Messages directly from Allah. The same angel whom Allah sent to Maryam," he said. "I wish I might live to see the day when your people turn you out, for never was any man who received Divine Revelation unopposed by his people. But if I live that long I shall certainly help you."

But it was not to be. Old and blind, Warqa bin Naufal died soon after.

Muhammad continued to visit the cave, but Jibril did not reappear. During that time, he grew spiritually stronger; but due to Jibril's absence, he began to fear he was not worthy of such a momentous task. Jibril's visits then resumed to reassure him that Allah had indeed chosen him to be a prophet.

The visits became more frequent until finally Jibril conveyed the formal command from Allah: "O you, Muhammad, wrapped in your garments. Arise and warn. And magnify your Lord. And purify your garments. And keep away from idols. And show not favour, seeking worldly gain. For the sake of thy Lord be patient." (Holy Qur'an, 74: 1)

Muhammad went home and told Khadijah who became the first person to believe in his prophethood. Later, when Allah commanded Muhammad to pray regularly, Khadijah would join him in prayer. One day, his cousin Ali, Abu Talib's son who also lived with them, saw them praying together.

"Why were you bowing your heads in this way?" he asked them.

"O Ali! We were bowing before Allah, Who has chosen me as a prophet and commanded me to call the people to follow Him," Muhammad answered. "Worship Allah and believe in my prophethood. Leave the worship of Lat and Manat and all the other idols."

Ali did not reply. This was such an astronomical revelation, he needed time to think. All night he tossed and turned in his bed, his mind searching for the truth. By morning, all doubts had vanished, and he declared his faith. Next to declare faith was Zaid, Kadijah's freed slave. Muhammad's very dear friend, Abu Bakr, was the first person outside the family to embrace Islam. Encouraged by Abu Bakr's declaration, Uthman, Zubair, Abdul Rahman bin Auf, Sa'd bin Abi Waqqas and Talha also accepted Islam.

Muhammad's mission of calling the people to the true religion, Islam, had begun, but only secretly. When the number of Muslims rose to more than thirty, Muhammad found a spacious house where all could gather and listen to his sermons. Gradually, more people embraced Islam including a considerable number of Quraysh.

Desperate to stop Muhammad, the pagan Quraysh began persecuting the believers. Those who escaped death or torture suffered great hardships, but none renounced their new-found faith. Their belief in Allah, and His promise of a place in Paradise for those who followed Him, gave them immense patience and strength. Deeply concerned for their well-being and safety, Muhammad gave them permission to migrate to Abyssinia. The King of Abyssinia was a good Christian, so Muhammad was sure he would offer them his protection.

When the Quraysh came to know that a group of Muslims had secretly left for Abyssinia they were furious and sent a group of men to find them. They demanded their immediate return, but the king was no fool. He called the Muslims to his court and asked them about this nascent religion they called Islam.

"O king!" one of them said. "We used to believe in useless stone idols. And we used to lie and cheat and commit the most atrocious crimes. Then Allah sent His Prophet to us. He teaches us nothing but truth, justice, and goodness. The Quraysh only want us back so they can persecute us again."

The king then called the Quraysh to his court. "Go home!" he told them. "These Muslims are welcome to live peacefully in my kingdom."

From then onwards, Muhammad's life was in danger. While some clansmen supported him out of tribal loyalty, despite their disbelief in his mission, most refused to give up their self-made gods and idols and became his arch enemies. Strange as it may seem, the Quraysh believed in Allah as the God of Ibrahim, and acknowledged Him as their Creator and Provider, but had the weird misconception they could only worship Him through their gods and idols.

For fear of persecution, even death, the Makkan converts still had to hide their adherence to Islam. Muhammad, however, began to worship and pray openly, even in the presence of those who fiercely opposed him. Utaibah bin Abi Lahab once approached him and rudely shouted, "I do not believe in you and the Qur'an!"

He then got hold of Muhammad, tore his shirt, and spat on him. Another disbeliever, Uqbah bin Abi Mu'ait, once stood behind Muhammad while he was praying. When he bowed in prostration, Uqbah put his foot on his neck and pressed as hard as he could. On another occasion, again when Muhammad was prostrating, he threw the guts of a camel on his back. Uqbah and his friends burst into raucous laughter, but Muhammad did not raise his head. When his beloved daughter, Fatimah, heard what had happened, she rushed to his aid and removed the vile-smelling offal.

Even his neighbours, some of whom were also his relatives, took delight in tormenting him. Abu Lahab was one of them. His real name was Abd al-Uzza, but he was better known by his nickname, Abu Lahab, which means *Father of the Flame*, a name given to him because he had a very red face. Despite being Muhammad's paternal uncle, he was his archenemy. He would not only insult him but throw stones at his ankles until they bled.

As for Lahab's foul-tongued wife, Umm Jamil-bint-Harb, she made it her mission to compose hate poems and spread wicked rumours about Muhammad. She would also tie bundles of thorny sticks together with woven strands of palm leaves and spread them along the paths he walked. But Muhammad had genuine love and compassion for all, and never complained against those who harmed him or showed disrespect.

It was in the sixth year of his prophethood that Muhammad felt the pressing need to win over the support of someone powerful and influential in Makkah, so he prayed, "O Allah! Give strength to Islam through either of two men you love more, Umar bin Al-Khattab or Abu Jahl bin Hisham."

Soon after, Muhammad's uncle, Hamzah, who commanded a prominent position of respect and authority in Makkan society, embraced Islam; and just three days after that, Umar bin Al-Khattab also converted. It was like a miracle and the answer to Muhammad's prayer. Umar was highly respected among the people of Makkah and a man of supreme courage, but he had an explosive temper. From the beginning, he had been a bitter opponent of the Prophet.

On the day of his conversion, Umar had set out ranting with rage, sword drawn, determined to kill Muhammad. On the way, however, he was stopped by Nu'aim bin Abdullah, who asked him where he was going in such haste.

"To kill that man, Muhammad," he bellowed.

"Why don't you take care of your own family first and set them right," Nu'aim advised.

He then told him the startling news that his sister and her family had secretly embraced Islam. As Umar drew near his sister's house, he could hear the recitation of the Holy Qur'an. Enraged, he rushed inside, lunged at his brother-in-law, but struck his sister on the head instead as she tried to protect her husband. The sight of the blood streaming down his dear sister's face melted Umar's heart. He then asked them what they had been reciting.

"Verily, I am Allah! None has the right to be worshipped but I, so worship Me and maintain prayer for My remembrance," his sister recited.

With a look of fiery resolve and sword held high, Umar raced to the house in Safa where Muhammad held his secret meetings. Muhammad's companions saw him approaching and, fearing he had come to kill their beloved Prophet, rushed forward to close the door on him.

Muhammad intervened. "Let him come in," he said.

To everyone's surprise, Umar declared his belief in the Messenger and his Message from the Lord. Overjoyed, Muhammad and his companions shouted, *"Allahu Akbar!"* (Allah is the Greatest) so loudly, it was heard far off in the Kaaba. Muhammad then gave Umar the title, al-Farooq, which means, *'he who distinguishes truth from falsehood.'*

As for Abu Jahl bin Hisham, the prominent leader whose support to strengthen his mission Muhammad had prayed for, he remained his archenemy and fierce opponent of Islam till the day he died in the Battle of Badr. Two young Ansar boys, who had sworn to kill him because he used to abuse Allah's Messenger, singled him out and slew him.

The news of Muhammad's mission travelled like a sweet breeze to every corner of the city and far beyond. Finally, Muhammad received the command from Allah to call the people openly to his religion, so he invited all his relatives to a feast and delivered a sermon urging them to leave their idols and embrace Islam. His uncle, Abu Lahab, who was still a staunch idol-worshipper, was furious. Shouting abuse, he stormed out of the meeting, taking others with him.

Undaunted, Muhammad later invited Abdul Muttalib's entire clan to a feast. When he spoke, urging them to follow him and accept Islam, there was pin-drop silence. Surprisingly, Ali, who was just a youth, stood up and openly declared he would follow Muhammad and stand by him. Although everyone laughed at him at the time, the young lad's boldness made them think earnestly about Muhammad's Message.

Muhammad had proclaimed his Message to secret gatherings, to relatives and clansmen. Now it was time to proclaim it publicly in an open place. So, early one morning, he climbed to the top of Saffa and shouted, *"Ya Sabahah!"* Calamity of the morning! A cry the Arabs used to draw attention to danger or approaching invaders.

Immediately, people came running out of their houses to find out who was calling and why. It sounded like Muhammad's voice, so people from all the Quraysh families rushed to Saffa, anxious to know what danger was threatening them. Turning to the crowd that had gathered, Muhammad asked: "Would you believe me if I told you there is an army behind this hill, ready to attack you?"

"Yes, we would believe you," they readily replied. "We have never heard you tell a lie."

"If you believe me then listen to what I have to say. I am Allah's Messenger. Allah is One. He alone is God. None of your idols or images is a real god. Allah is our Creator. He gave us life. When we die we shall return to Him. He will give us life again and will judge us. So, give up your idols, leave your evil ways and believe in Him alone."

"Did you call us for this? May you perish forever! May you die!" Abu Lahab shouted.

Shaken by his uncle's outburst, Muhammad could not understand why he so vehemently opposed him. Later, when surah al-Masad was revealed, Allah told Muhammad: "The power of Abu Lahab will perish. His wealth and gains will not exempt him. He will be plunged into flaming fire." Holy Qur'an, 111: 1.

As Muhammad continued his preaching, the Quraysh became increasingly agitated. They devised daring but futile plans to kill him. Abu Jahl intended to drop a rock on his head while he was praying in the sanctuary of the Kaaba, but as he approached the Prophet carrying a huge rock, he suddenly turned back, his hands trembling so much the rock fell to the ground. People rushed forward, wanting to know what had happened.

"When I got close to Muhammad, an odd-looking camel with fearsome canine teeth suddenly appeared and it was about to devour me," he told them.

How to put an end to Muhammad's preaching? This was the Quraysh's quandary, and they were running out of ideas. They decided to appeal to Abu Talib. Knowing Muhammad dearly loved and respected him and would do anything to please him, they would discuss the matter with him in the hope he could persuade his nephew to give up his crazy mission.

"We can no longer tolerate what Muhammad is preaching," they told him. "It is an insult to all our deities as well as to our ancestors."

When they were alone together, Abu Talib tried to reason with Muhammad. "The Quraysh are too powerful," he warned him. "You cannot fight them and win."

Muhammad's faith was unshakable. "By Allah!" he declared. "Even if the people of Makkah put the sun in my right hand and the moon in my left, I will never abandon my mission. I will either complete it or die in the attempt."

Abu Talib realised it was impossible to stop Muhammad, and although he did not openly accept Islam, he offered his nephew his full support and protection. Muhammad continued his mission, and more people turned to Islam; and the more Muhammad's followers grew in number, the more unsettled the Quraysh became. They knew they were losing control. People no longer listened to them. They listened to Muhammad.

So, they sent Utbah to bargain with him. "O Muhammad!" he said. "We have decided to make you a reasonable offer. If you stop talking against our gods, we will give you whatever you want. If you want to be the king of Makkah, we will make you our king. If you want to marry a beautiful woman, we will find the most beautiful woman for you. If you want to be rich, we will give you as much as you want. If you are mentally ill, we will get the best doctors to treat you. And if you are possessed by evil spirits, we will find someone to cure you. We are ready to do anything if you agree to stop preaching against our gods and our religion."

In reply, Muhammad recited verses of the Holy Qur'an. Utbah then realised that any attempt to deter Muhammad from his chosen path was futile. He would never give up his mission. When he told this to the Quraysh chiefs, they were livid. United in their determination to rid themselves of Muhammad, they held a meeting where all swore an oath and signed a contract declaring that until the Prophet was given over to them to be killed, they would cease all business dealings, inter-marriage, social contact, and verbal communication with the tribes of Banu Hashim and Banu al-Muttalib, the two tribes of the prophet's family who had pledged to protect him. They fixed the treaty to the wall of the Kaaba for all to see.

The life of every Muslim in Makkah was now in such grave danger, Abu Talib decided to withdraw to a hilly gorge on the eastern outskirts of Makkah. The two tribes joined them; and there Muhammad and his followers were confined for three long years. It became known as the Valley of Abu Talib. Since traders were not allowed to sell goods and provisions to anyone from the Valley of Abu Talib, Muhammad and his followers were often on the verge of starvation. But for the grace of Allah and the courageous sympathisers who smuggled in food whenever they could, all would have perished.

In the month of Muharram, the tenth year of Muhammad's mission, the treaty that had caused their incarceration was finally rescinded, thanks to sympathisers who put pressure on the Quraysh to nullify the pact. Abu Jahl, however, was still arguing with them and insisting the treaty should remain when Abu Talib arrived with a special message. Muhammad had received a revelation that every word of the treaty had been eaten away by ants, except the name of Allah.

"If this proves untrue, I shall give Muhammad over to you," he vowed. "But if it is true, then you must withdraw all sanctions and put an end to the boycott."

They all agreed and went to inspect the parchment. As revealed to Muhammad, ants had eaten through it. All that remained was the part bearing the name of Allah. Once again, the Prophet's life was spared, and the two tribes were free to go back to their homes. It turned out that their long incarceration was a blessing for Islam. When people further abroad heard of the persecution and brave endurance of Muhammad and his followers, they also entered the fold of Islam.

The Quraysh soon renewed their cruel oppression of the Muslims, and Abu Talib continued to protect and defend his nephew. However, he was now an old man in his eighties and of frail health. In the month of Rajab, the tenth year of Muhammad's prophethood, Abu Talib died. A few months later, Khadijah also died. With the death of Abu Talib, Muhammad lost an uncle, a friend and staunch supporter. With the death of Khadijah, he lost a noble, virtuous wife whose love and devotion endeared her as his closest, most loyal companion.

"She had faith in me when people rejected me," Muhammad once said about her. "She believed in me when the people disbelieved. She supported me with her wealth, and through her Allah blessed me with children."

Deeply grieved by the loss of the two people dearest to him, Muhammad called it the Year of Sorrow. It was an Arab custom for a man to have more than one wife, but during the twenty-five years he was married to Khadijah, Muhammad did not marry anyone else. However, after her death he needed someone to look after the home and the children, so in Shawwal of the same year he married a Muslim widow named Sawdah. Not long after, he married Aishah, the daughter of his closest friend, Abu Bakr. She was a young girl who had never been married before. Later, he took other wives, mostly widows; to provide them protection or to strengthen the faith by creating alliance between tribes.

Following the deaths of Abu Talib and Khadijah, the Quraysh's campaign of persecution intensified. At the same time, Allah commanded Muhammad to preach not only to the people of Arabia but to the entire world, so he started preaching in the camps of the caravans that came to Makkah. The Quraysh were completely flummoxed. Was there no way of silencing this man they now called a madman?

Muhammad decided to search for a safer place where he could preach in peace, so he left Makkah and went to the city of Ta'if. There, however, the people proved to be even worse. They made fun of him, hurled stones at him and drove him out of the city. As he was leaving, bruised, wounded, and bleeding, he took shelter in a garden and prayed, asking Allah to forgive the people of Ta'if and to give him strength. Ten years later, Allah answered the Prophet's prayer when the people of Ta'if embraced Islam.

One night, in the twelfth year of his prophethood when Muhammad was fifty-two years old, the Archangel Jibril came and woke him. He called him outside and together they mounted a white animal called Buraq, smaller than a pony and incredibly swift. It stopped at Medina where Jibril told Muhammad, "You will migrate to this place."

Next, Buraq stopped at Mount Tur, the place where Allah had spoken to Prophet Musa. And then it stopped at Bait-ul-Laham (Bethlehem), birthplace of Prophet Isa. Finally, it stopped at Masjid al-Aqsa in Jerusalem, and from a rock beside the mosque Muhammad was taken up and shown the Seven Heavens. In each of the Heavens he met the prophets who had come before him and led them all in prayer. He then ascended to the highest Heaven, a place where no angel or human being had ever been before. He was also shown Hell.

When he returned to Makkah his bed was still warm. He had travelled from Makkah to Jerusalem, countless miles away, and returned moments later, a miraculous event known as *Lailat al-Mi'raj*, the Night of the Ascension. But when

Muhammad told the Quraysh about this divine experience, they made fun of him.

"Two months journey in a single night! Impossible! Now we know for sure that you are mad."

Soon after this event, Muhammad was standing beside the Kaaba alongside a crowd of Quraysh when Allah displayed Jerusalem before him. He then described it in detail, verifying the fact that he had been there and that he was indeed a prophet. But still the Quraysh refused to believe. Nothing could ever convince them to leave their worthless idols and meaningless traditions. To them, this was not a revelation but humiliation.

In retaliation, they subjected the Muslims still living in Makkah to relentless persecution. Muhammad thus granted his followers permission to migrate to Medina. Surreptitiously, mostly under cover of darkness, small groups of Muslims began to leave the city. For so many, leaving home and family was distressing, the journey to Medina long and tedious, but the Ansar, the local inhabitants of Medina, offered them a warm welcome.

The Quraysh suddenly realized how threatened they were. A Muslim stronghold in Medina meant the trade route from Yemen to Syria would fall into the control of the Muslims. Desperate, and more determined than ever, the chiefs of all the tribes held a secret meeting to discuss a long-term solution; namely, to be rid of Muhammad.

Someone proposed they imprison him for life, but the others quickly dismissed this idea. Muhammad's followers were so devoted, they would risk their lives to set him free. When someone else suggested they exile him, that plan was also rejected. Muhammad would preach elsewhere and win the hearts of even more people. And with more followers on his side, he might invade Makkah and defeat the Quraysh altogether.

Finally, Abu Jahl decided there was no alternative but to kill him. This would finally put an end to their troubles. Unanimously, all agreed. They decided that to ensure the success of their plan, a group of men together would attack him at night while he was in his bed.

The day before the planned assassination, Jibril came to warn Muhammad. He told him not to sleep in his bed that night, and that the time had come for him to migrate to Medina. Muhammad immediately sent word to Abu Bakr to prepare for the long journey. He then called Ali and told him to sleep in his bed.

"No harm will come to you," he assured him. "Just cover yourself with my sheet."

At the appointed hour, the assassins came, but instead of implementing their original plan, they decided to wait outside the house and ambush Muhammad the moment he came out early in the morning. As they lay asleep, Muhammad walked past them completely unnoticed, quietly reciting verses of the Holy Qur'an. He went directly to Abu Bakr's house and hid there. When the assassins saw Ali rising from Muhammad's bed the following morning, they were dumbfounded.

Meanwhile, climbing through a window at the back of the house to avoid being seen, Muhammad and Abu Bakr set off towards the mountain of Thaur, south of Makkah on the road to Yemen; Medina being towards the north of Makkah on the road to Syria. Knowing the Quraysh would pursue them along the normal route northwards, their plan was to hide in a cave near the top of Mount Thaur until the search died down. Tired and footsore, they finally made the steep and difficult climb to the cave.

For as long as they stayed in the cave, Abu Bakr's freed slave grazed the sheep all day as usual, but at night he went to the cave with food and fresh milk and the latest reports of the enemy's movements. Abu Bakr's son, Abdullah, also brought news at night.

Realizing their plot had been thwarted, the Quraysh launched a frantic search along the route to Medina. Although they had experienced track guides to help them, they could find no trace of Muhammad, so they turned southwards. A group of them even climbed the mountain of Thaur and reached the cave, but a spider's web covered the entrance, a sign that no one was likely to be inside, so they hesitated. Should they explore the cave anyway, they wondered?

"What will you find in there?" one of them said. "This web looks as though it was woven ages ago, long before the birth of Muhammad."

A spider's web covering the entrance to the cave.

Inside the cave, Abu Bakr held his breath. He could see the men's feet, just inches away. "O Messenger of Allah!" he said in the slightest of whispers. "If one of them looks down he will see us."

Muhammad, perfectly calm, replied, "O Abu Bakr! Do not worry. Besides the two of us there is our third companion, Allah."

Convinced that no one could be in the cave, the scouts turned away and went back down the mountain. Completely baffled, the Quraysh continued their search, but after three days still had no clue as to Muhammad's whereabouts; and since Abu Bakr was also missing, they were convinced they were together, so they offered a reward of one hundred camels for each of them.

At night-time of the third day, Abu Bakr's family and his track guide arrived at the foot of Mount Thaur with camels and provisions for the long trek to Medina. When his followers in Medina received news that Muhammad was on his way to join them, they would sit on the roadside in the morning, eagerly awaiting his arrival, and return to their homes at noon when the heat became unbearable.

On the 8th of Rabi-ul-Awwal, Muhammad finally entered Quba, a valley three miles south of Medina. The Ansar and Muhajreen (immigrants) who had been waiting for him had gone home, but a Jew who had climbed onto his roof to repair it, spotted the Prophet. Arousing everyone from their mid-day slumber, he cried out, "Your chief whom you eagerly await has come."

Although Muhammad was still far away, the excited devotees rushed to greet him. After a brief stay in Quba, he finally entered Medina. The city resounded with shouts of jubilation and songs of welcome. Eagerly, they rushed forward to lead the Prophet's camel, but the Prophet had given her free rein to go in whatever direction Allah guided her. She stopped at the house of Abu Ayyub Ansari who heartily welcomed the honoured guest.

Muhammad's first task in Medina was to build a mosque; the next was to establish true friendship and fraternity between the Muhajreen and the Ansar. He brought both groups together and gave the hand of one Muhajir into the hand of one Ansar and made them brothers. With genuine affection and generosity, the Ansar shared their wealth and property with their Muslim brothers. Next, Muhammad settled the age-old feud between the two well-known Ansar tribes, the Aus and Khazraj. All the Muslims of Medina became one party, the Party of Allah.

Islam now had a firm foothold in the Arabian Peninsula, which the Quraysh construed as a serious threat to their supremacy. The Muslims of Medina were now in real danger of attack from the Quraysh. They also faced hostility from the Jews. Astutely, Muhammad entered a peace treaty with the Jews of Medina and outlying settlements. According to the various clauses of the treaty, Muhammad would not fight them, and they would not fight him, nor would they join forces with those who fought the Muslims; and if anyone attacked the Jews, the Muslims would assist them.

One of the signatories of this treaty was the tribe of Banu Nadir. However, it soon became apparent that they were not trustworthy. In fact, they were hypocrites and traitors. Descendants of Prophet Harun, they were well versed in the Holy Scripture, the Taurat (Torah), and knew it prophesied the coming of Allah's Messenger; and although they recognized from the signs and descriptions that Muhammad was indeed the Messenger it foretold, they refused to accept it.

The migration of Allah's Messenger to Medina had also been foretold in the Taurat, which was the very reason they had left their homes in Syria, hoping to be the first to welcome him. So how was it possible, they argued, that the Promised One was not from their clan but a descendent of Ismail? Seething with jealousy and rage, they refused to acknowledge Muhammad as Allah's Messenger.

Although they had pledged to uphold the terms of the treaty, in private the Banu Nadir plotted against Muhammad and his followers, their smooth tongue cleverly concealing the resentment in their hearts. They politely requested Muhammad to send a band of Muslims to preach the religion of Islam. Muhammad eagerly responded by dispatching seventy of his noble Companions. It proved, however, to be an artful, wicked conspiracy. They mercilessly killed them all, except one.

Secretly, the Banu Nadir had allied with the Quraysh to annihilate the Muslims. They also schemed to kill Muhammad. Following the massacre of the noble Companions, the Prophet went immediately to confront them. They asked him to wait outside, so he sat down, leant against a wall, and waited. Their plan was for someone to climb to the top of the wall from the other side and drop a rock on his head. However, forewarned by Allah, Muhammad left before they could execute their diabolical plan.

Time and again, the Banu Nadir violated the terms of the treaty and proved beyond doubt that they were a treacherous, malicious threat to the Muslims of Medina. Muhammad thus issued immediate orders for their exile and gave them ten days to return to Syria.

Over the next few years, serious battles were fought, and by Allah's will most were victorious. Unlike other historical battles, the purpose of which was to subjugate or annihilate people for expansion of territory, power and control, the Muslims' battles were solely to purge Arabia of idolatry, to defeat those who hindered and persecuted the believers and to promote the Message of Islam.

The Muslim army thus grew from strength to strength, in numbers and in faith. Muhammad employed new, effective strategies, and imposed battle regulations that proved to be the most equitable laws ever devised. His army fought only opposing armies, soldier against soldier. To harm anyone engaged in prayer in their place of worship, to plunder, kill a woman, child, or elderly person, to destroy crops, orchards, or green trees – all were forbidden; injunctions that clearly reflect the magnitude of Muhammad's compassion and his desire to bring about reforms in all aspects of life.

One last battle remained. To conquer the Sacred House of Allah, the Holy Kaaba, which was still in the custody of the polytheists who had turned it into the centre of idolatry. Muhammad decided it was now time to take control, remove all the idols and purify the Kaaba for the worship of Allah alone. He thus ordered his men to prepare for a long journey but kept the purpose of the expedition a closely guarded secret.

On 10th Ramadhan, 8 Hijri, the Muslim army gathered and marched towards Makkah. Along the way, men from various tribes whom Muhammad had previously ordered to be at the ready joined them. They neither knew where they were going nor the objective but, enthused by the confidence that with Muhammad as their Commander-in-Chief no one could defeat them, all were ready and willing to fight.

When night came, the army of about ten thousand men settled in the vast desert area outside Makkah. It was customary for a group of soldiers to share one campfire, but Muhammad ordered every single soldier to light a fire. From far off, the army would appear to be much larger than it was because the enemy would estimate its size according to the number of fires. The ruse worked. When the tribes on the distant hills of Makkah saw the huge stretch of fires illuminating the night sky, they were convinced the Muslims were about to invade Makkah with an army of at least fifty thousand strong.

However, it was not Muhammad's intention to fight, but to enter the city peacefully without any battle, inspired by a dream he had in which he saw himself and his companions entering Makkah with heads shaved or cut short. And that is exactly what happened. Convinced that Muhammad's army was so formidable he stood no chance of defeating it, Abu Sufyan ibn Harb, leader of the Quraysh, surrendered. The Muslim army then entered Makkah with no resistance.

Muhammad went directly to the Kaaba and struck down all the idols, reciting the following: "O Prophet! Say to the people: Truth has come. Falsehood has vanished; and falsehood had to vanish." (Holy Qur'an, 17: 81)

When he had purged the Kaaba of all impurities, the Prophet ordered Bilal to ascend the roof of the Kaaba and announce Adhan, the call to prayer. Bilal was an Abyssinian, formerly the slave of a disbeliever in Makkah. After he had embraced Islam, the Quraysh tortured him by forcing him to lie down on the burning sand under the midday sun. Placing a heavy stone on his chest so that he could not move, they urged him to renounce Islam. Each time they repeated this punishment, in an attempt to force him to renounce Islam, Bilal would shout, *"Ahad!"* meaning, One (Allah is One)! Only when Abu Bakr paid for his manumission did the torture stop, and his life was spared.

Bilal had such a melodious voice that whenever he gave Adhan the peoples' hearts filled with emotion, and tears would flow down their cheeks. The Adhan over, Muhammad then led the Muslims in prayer. A large congregation of worshippers, many of whom were the very Quraysh who for years had mercilessly pursued and persecuted the Prophet and his followers, filled the spacious compound of the Kaaba. After the prayer, he delivered the following sermon:

"There is no God save Allah and He has no partner. He has fulfilled His promise. He aided His Servant. He alone defeated all armies. Listen! This day, all pride and arrogance, all blood feuds, blood wit, demand of goods, I trample under my foot, but the guardianship of the House of Allah and the offering of water to pilgrims, they remain. I confirm those currently in these offices. O' Quraysh! Allah has now obliterated pride and family privileges of the period of ignorance. All humans are offspring of Adam, and Adam was created from clay."

What happened thereafter was nothing short of a miracle. From near and far, people flocked to Arabia to join Muhammad's faith. His life's mission now accomplished, just one thing remained, a farewell pilgrimage. Standing on the crest of Jabal-ul-Arafat, Muhammad addressed the multitude of Muslims gathered there. The following is an excerpt but main content of his sermon:

"O People! Listen to what I have to say for I do not know how long I will remain among you. Your lives and your property are sacred and inviolable amongst one another until you appear before your Lord, as this day and this month is sacred for all. And remember, you will have to appear before your Lord Who shall demand from you an account of all your actions ... You have rights over your wives and your wives have rights over you ... so treat them with kindness.

"As for your slaves, feed them such food as you eat yourself and clothe them with the same clothes you wear. And if they do anything wrong, which you are not inclined to forgive, then part with them, for they are the servants of your Lord and must not be treated harshly. Know that all Muslims are brothers, and you are one brotherhood. Nothing that belongs to another is lawful unto his brother unless feely given out of goodwill. Guard yourself against committing injustice."

With the following words Muhammad ended his final address: "O Lord! I have delivered the Message and completed my work. I beseech Thee, O Lord, to bear witness unto it."

Muhammad spent the last year of his life in Medina. On the evening of Monday, 12 Rabi-ul-Awwal, 11th Hijra (8 June, 632 C.E.) after a short illness, Prophet Muhammad died.

The dreadful news of his death was like a tsunami, engulfing the city in a tide of grief. Totally stunned, most refused to believe it. But it was true. In his private chamber, with his head resting on the lap of his beloved wife, Aishah, Muhammad had breathed his last.

There might have been chaos, but Abu Bakr, himself deeply shaken with grief, rallied everyone with these words: "O people! He who worshipped Muhammad should know that Muhammad is dead. But as for him who worshipped Allah, it is a fact that Allah lives and knows not death."

He then recited, "Muhammad is but a Messenger, Messengers (the like of whom) have passed away before him. Will it be that when he dies or is killed you will turn back on your heels? He who turns back on his heels does no harm to Allah; and Allah will reward the thankful." (Holy Qur'an, 3: 144)

Prophet Muhammad, sallallhu alayhi wasallam, is buried where he breathed his last, a short distance from his pulpit in al Masjid an-Nabawi, in the Arabian city of Medina.

Author's Comments

Muhammad's life was fraught with all manner of difficulties, as were the lives of all the noble Messengers, but by Allah's Will he overcame them all. He fought and won numerous battles against his fiercest enemies, and through various treaties and alliances brought peace to the once warring tribes of Arabia. He eradicated ignorance and idol worship and established Islam.

Islam means peace. It also means submission to the Will of God. But to submit, man must control his inner self, his psyche ego, which for ordinary men is far from easy. It was, however, a quality all the noble Messengers possessed. It was never beneath Muhammad's dignity, even when the whole of Arabia was under his command, to consult with his companions, share meals with servants, and perform menial tasks. He was undeniably the most illustrious leader, yet he walked alongside his followers with shoulders slightly bent in humility. He not only preached equality and fraternity; he practised it.

Unlike most men, reproof did not ruffle or offend him. He once made an error for which Allah admonished him openly by revealing verses 1–11, of surah 80, Abasa (He Frowned):

"He frowned and turned away because the blind man came to him. What could inform you that he might grow in grace or take heed and so the reminder might have benefitted him? As for him who thinks himself independent, to him you pay regard. Yet it is not your concern if he grows not in grace. But as for him who comes to you with earnest purpose and fears God, from him you are distracted. Nay, but verily it is an admonishment."

These verses refer to the occasion Muhammad was conversing with a high-ranking Quraysh, a non-believer, trying to convince him of the truth of Islam. A blind man interrupted and asked a question regarding the faith, but Muhammad frowned at him and without answering turned his attention again to the Quraysh man. Allah then reprimanded Muhammad and explained that regardless of his efforts the Quraysh man was never going to believe, whereas the blind man was genuinely seeking guidance and was more deserving of his attention.

Muhammad's reason for giving his attention to the high-ranking Quraysh was not to gain any personal favour, but the hope that winning him over to Islam would encourage others to follow. However, on this occasion Muhammad misjudged. We all tend to judge others or assess situations, often wrongly, whereas Allah knows best.

Muhammad was the epitome of compassion. It was one of the pivotal forces that guided him and enabled him to win the hearts of his staunchest enemies. It troubled him to see anyone in pain or difficulty, even those like Abu Lahab and his wife, Umm Jamil, who taunted and abused him at every opportunity.

"Verily, there has come to you a Messenger from amongst yourselves. It grieves him that you should receive any injury or difficulty. He is anxious about you (to be rightly guided), and for the believers he is full of pity, kind and merciful." Holy Qur'an, 9: 128.

He prayed for those who refused to accept Islam, even wept for them, because he knew the dreadful doom that awaited them, but Allah sent surah 6, al-An'am (The Cattle), verse 107, to comfort and reassure him that he was not responsible for their lack of faith: "We have not set you as a keeper over them, nor are you responsible for them."

Muhammad was also the personification of Integrity. He always spoke the truth and his promises were binding. He once told his followers that there are four signs of a hypocrite: whenever he speaks, he tells a lie; whenever he makes a promise, he breaks it; whenever someone trusts him, he betrays that trust; and whenever he is angry, he uses abusive language.

Like all the noble Messengers, Muhammad was guided by Divine Inspiration. It was constant guidance from Almighty Allah that moulded him into the most perfect of men for all humanity to emulate. Allah instructed, commanded, reminded, reprimanded, comforted, and reassured him every step of the way. Sometimes, He openly commended him.

"And by the Mercy of Allah, you dealt with them gently. And had you been harsh they would have turned away from you and dispersed." Holy Qur'an, 3: 159.

All too often, we are harsh with others and then wonder why they stop listening to us and drift away, preferring the company of others. Harshness drives people away. Love and compassion draw them closer.

When Muhammad was born into this world women were treated like chattel, to be bartered and used at will. Baby girls were often buried alive because they were considered a burden and a disgrace. A champion of women's rights, Muhammad changed all that. He elevated women from the position of slaves to one of respect and dignity. There were laws to protect them. One entire surah of the Holy Qur'an, *al-Nisa*, the Women, deals with laws and directives regarding women.

He once said, "The believers who show the most perfect faith are those who have the best morals, and the best of you are those who are the best to their wives."

In his farewell sermon, he reminded the men folk of their duty towards women: "You have rights over your wives and your wives have rights over you ... so treat them with kindness."

Like all prophets, Muhammad practised what he preached. It is testament to his exemplary behaviour towards his wives that when he offered them a choice, freedom to leave him for a life of comfort or to remain and share his frugal life, they unanimously chose to stay.

Yet again, regarding women's rights, we have upset the balance. While in some places women's authority has been raised to an unprecedented level, in many countries women are more akin to slaves. Lack of respect for women adversely affects family life, the family being the fabric of society. It thus follows that only those nations can hope to thrive where women are afforded their rights, due respect, and protection.

Prophet Muhammad taught fairness, equality, and moderation. An exemplar for all humanity, he set the bar of excellence in all avenues of life. His understanding of the human mind and human nature would astound any modern-day professor of behavioural sciences. It was this acumen, together with his complete truthfulness and genuine love and compassion for his fellow beings that enabled him to win the hearts of his fiercest opponents, thereby spreading Islam.

He was also an advocate of human rights. When he exposed the Banu Nadir for their endless conspiracies, Muhammad showed no maliciousness towards them. There was no massacre, no plundering. He only demanded that they evacuate the town and return to Syria to live in exile. He even allowed them to take all their wealth and belongings with them, whatever they could load onto their camels and other beasts of burden.

Without doubt, to follow the teachings of Prophet Muhammad and to express the utmost respect for him is intrinsic to Islam. From the highest minarets of the world, no less than five times a day, his name resounds in the Adhan, the call to prayer. In the prayer itself, Muslims mention his blessed name and pray for him; and in the Sacred Book that was revealed to him over a period of twenty-three years, the Holy Qur'an, his name is frequently mentioned alongside the name of Almighty Allah.

In the Holy Qur'an, 33: 56, Allah Himself says: "Allah sends His salat (honour, blessings, mercy) on the Prophet, and His angels (ask Allah to bless and forgive him). O you who believe! Send your salat (ask Allah to bless him) and greet him with the Islamic way of greeting (Asalamu-alaikum)."

The following Hadith by Sahih Bukhari, also affirms that Muhammad is worthy of the highest honour and respect. When one of his followers asked him how they should greet him, he told him to say:

"ALLAH HUMMA SALLI ALA MUHAMMADIN WA'ALA ALI MUHAMMADIN, KAMA SALAITA ALA IBRAHIMA WA ALA ALI IBRAHIMA, INNAKA HAMIDUN MAJEED. ALLAHUMMA BARIK ALA MUHAMMADIN WA ALA ALI MUHAMMADIN KAMA BARAKTA ALA IBRAHIMA WA ALA ALI IBRAHIMA, INNAKA HAMIDUN MAJEED."

O Allah! Send Your salat on Muhammad and on the family or followers of Muhammad, as You sent Your salat on Ibrahim and the family or followers of Ibrahim, for You are the Most Praiseworthy, the Most Glorious. O Allah! Send Your blessings on Muhammad and on the family or followers of Muhammad, as You sent Your blessings on Ibrahim and the family or followers of Ibrahim, for You are the Most Praiseworthy, the Most Glorious.

Islam relates to every-day affairs. It reinforces our understanding of right and wrong and clarifies our perception of moral, religious, and social obligations. It has the power to spiritually enlighten those who faithfully follow it. And as Allah tells us in the Holy Qur'an, 5: 3, it is the perfect religion: "This day, I have perfected your religion for you, completed my favour upon you, and have chosen Islam for you as your religion."

Journey's End

To end our journey, here is a parable attributed to Prophet Muhammad. ﷺ

A Grateful Man

There were three poor companions belonging to the same tribe, Bani Israel. One was a leper; one was bald; and one was blind. Allah wished to test them, so he sent an angel to each one in turn.

The angel first went to the leper and asked, "What do you wish for more than anything else?"

"Good complexion and good skin," the leper replied. "People despise me because I am a leper."

The angel touched him, and by the grace of Allah his skin became perfectly healthy and clear.

"Now," said the angel, "what would you like to own more than anything else?"

"Camels," the man replied.

Lo and behold! The angel presented him with a she-camel that was due to give birth to a calf. "May Allah bless you and your camel," said the angel as he went on his way.

Next, the angel came to the bald man and asked him, "What do you wish for more than anything else?"

"I wish to be cured of my baldness and to have nice hair," was his reply. "People despise me and make fun of me because of my bald head."

The angel touched the man's head, and by the grace of Allah it was instantly covered with healthy hair.

"Now," said the angel, "what would you like to own more than anything else?"

"Cows," the man replied.

Lo and behold! The angel presented him with a cow that was due to give birth to a calf. "May Allah bless you and your cow," said the angel as he went on his way.

The angel then went to the blind man and asked him the same question he had asked the others.

"I wish that Allah may restore my sight that I may see again," was the blind man's reply.

The angel touched the blind man's eyes and immediately, by the grace of Allah, he was able to see.

"Now," said the angel, "what would you like to own more than anything else?"

"Sheep," the man replied.

And lo and behold! The angel presented him with a ewe that was due to give birth to a lamb. The angel then left him and went on his way.

Soon after, the she-camel, the cow and the ewe gave birth to their young ones. They were healthy and sturdy. They matured and then multiplied so abundantly that the man who had been a leper had a large herd of camels occupying an entire valley; the man who had been bald had a large herd of cattle that filled another valley; and the man who was blind had a huge flock of sheep that occupied yet another valley.

One day, the angel, disguised as a leper, went to the camel owner. "I am destitute," the angel said. "During my journey, I have lost everything I had. No one can help me, except Allah and then you. So I ask you, in the Name of Allah, Who has given you such fair and healthy skin and so much wealth, to give me just one camel so that I may continue my journey and reach my destination."

"I cannot give you anything," the man curtly replied. "I already have too many obligations."

The angel was about to leave, but then turned back. "Wait!" he said. "I know you! Weren't you the leper whom everyone despised? And weren't you also a poor man before Allah gave you a pregnant camel?"

"No!" lied the man. "That's not true. I inherited this herd from my ancestors."

"If you are telling lies," said the angel, "then may Allah make you as you were before." And he went on his way.

Then, disguised as a bald man, the angel came to the owner of the herd of cattle and told him the same story about being destitute, having lost all his possessions during his travels.

"No one can help me, except Allah and then you. So I ask you, in the Name of Allah, Who has given you such lovely black hair and blessed you with so much wealth, to give me just one cow to help me continue my journey and reach my destination."

The man flatly refused and made lame excuses.

The angel took a step closer. "Don't I know you!" he said. "Weren't you once despised and ridiculed because you were bald? And weren't you also a poor man before Allah gave you a pregnant cow?"

"No! Certainly not! I inherited this herd of cattle from my ancestors," he curtly replied.

"If you are telling lies," said the angel, "then may Allah make you as you were before." And he went on his way.

Finally, disguised as a blind man, the angel came to the owner of the flock of sheep. He related the same story and asked him, in the Name of Allah, to give him just one sheep.

With true compassion for the blind stranger, the sheep owner replied, "Take whatever you wish. I was once blind, but Allah gave me back my sight. And I was poor, but Allah blessed me with a pregnant ewe from which I now have this huge flock of sheep. It is Allah who gives to whom He pleases, and I am profoundly grateful. So please, for Allah's sake, feel welcome to take whatever you may need for your journey."

"Keep your sheep," replied the angel. "This was Allah's way of testing you and He is truly pleased with you. As for the other two men who were once your companions, they have earned Allah's displeasure."

So saying, the angel disappeared.

About the author

S. J. Sear is British by birth, born in the beautiful Wiltshire countryside and educated in suburban London. Soon after leaving grammar school to pursue a teaching career, she converted to Islam. A few years later, after her marriage to a Pakistani Muslim, she migrated to Pakistan where she spent most of her adult life bringing up her children and working for a prestigious publishing house as editor-cum-writer of children's books. She is currently living in the UK, and although retired, continues to write books for children.

Printed in the United States
by Baker & Taylor Publisher Services